D0375017

What people are saying about *The Leadership Triangle:*

"*The Leadership Triangle* effectively illustrates how the role of the 'transformational leader' is increasingly important in today's world. No longer can we afford to lead with a one-size-fits-all mentality and expect to succeed or contribute on a professional/ personal basis. This terrific book offers clear and precise 'options' that a leader can choose in order to successfully transform their organization to meet the challenges of these uncertain times. It also provides many insightful examples from key leaders who model these concepts themselves. The result is a powerful read."

Stephen M. R. Covey, author of *The New York Times* and # 1 Wall Street Journal best seller, *The Speed of Trust*

"I love this book! I'm a firm believer in a situational approach to leadership. You not only need to use different strokes for different folks, but also for different situations. Ford and Tucker do a superb job of the latter scenario. *The Leadership Triangle* is a guidebook to help leaders, no matter what kind of organization, choose the right approach for the situation they face. Read this book and increase tenfold your chances of success."

Ken Blanchard, coauthor of *The One Minute Manager®* and *Leading at a Higher Level*

The Leadership Triangle

by
Kevin Ford and Ken Tucker

Intermedia Publishing Group

The Leadership Triangle

Published by:
Intermedia Publishing, Inc.
P.O. Box 2825
Peoria, Arizona 85380
www.intermediapub.com

ISBN 978-1-935906-76-6

Dedication

We dedicate this book to our friend and colleague,
the "soul" of TAG Consulting: Joe Jurkowski.

Table of Contents

Acknowledgements

We want to first thank our partners and associates at TAG Consulting. The principles in this book emerge from our collective thinking as an organization. We are also grateful to Tom Cousins, Chuck Knapp, and Shirley Franklin who have inspired us to see leadership in new ways. We are also indebted to some great leaders who made time to talk with us. Thanks to Truett Cathey, Steve Reinemund, Pete Coors, Ken Blanchard, Charles Handy, Frances Hesselbein, Norm Miller, David Hodge, Patrick Thompson, and many others who offered their insights and support.

Todd Hahn put the words together. He engaged in the interviews with the East Lake crew. He worked tirelessly as the foreman to pull this whole thing together. Todd is a gifted writer, thinker, and speaker. He saved us countless hours.

Our families have been incredibly supportive as we have worked diligently for over a year to bring this book to life.

Without our clients, this book would be primarily theoretical. But since we work with clients on a daily basis, we have been able to apply the principles in this book in very practical ways.

But ultimately… To God be the Glory!

Kevin and Ken

Introduction

David Allen

Best-Selling Author, *Getting Things Done*

In our work at the David Allen Company, we spend a lot of time in the intersection between the sublime and the simple, relative to productivity. Often in our field, the most powerful concepts, techniques, and methods are the most basic and obvious. But the key is usage—in the real world by real people about real stuff. Figuring out how to take simple, powerful principles and apply them to individual and organizational life is in many ways the focus of my life's work, and it is the driving force behind the Getting Things Done (GTD) methodology.

That is why I am delighted to recommend Kevin Ford and Kenneth Tucker's *The Leadership Triangle*. Ford and Tucker bring a lifetime of sophisticated and innovative thought to the subject of leadership. But their work as consultants demands that they keep their thought simple and accessible. *The Leadership Triangle* does this brilliantly and elegantly—with real style.

If you are a corporate or not-for-profit leader or simply want to lead better in your charitable and volunteer roles, there is much wisdom here for you. You will learn how to diagnose the type of leadership dilemmas you face, how to categorize your possible response, and then—practically—how to lead with skill and courage. Along the way, you will meet great leaders from all walks of life who have exemplified the principles of the book.

Whether you are an experienced leader looking for a primer or a novice to the art of leadership looking for a ready reference, you will find wise, practical, and engaging guides in Ford and Tucker.

Introduction

This is a book about leadership, but it may be unlike any leadership book you have ever read! Together, we are going to challenge some common assumptions about what leadership is and how you can practice it. You are going to receive some new tools that will help you to lead effectively in even the most challenging environments. You'll be challenged to rethink much of what you have been taught about leadership in the past. And you'll be stretched to dream of the long-term, positive impact you can make in your world!

This is a book for leaders of all types, regardless of position or industry. It is for business leaders, to be sure. But it is also for teachers, coaches, pastors, chairpersons of not-for-profit boards, and even parents. If you lead at any level in your life, this book is for you.

In our work as consultants and thought leaders we are around a lot of leaders. It is our privilege to coach, counsel and advise leaders and soon-to-be leaders from all sorts of industries in all sorts of settings. We've learned a lot and we continue to learn more every day. We've discovered along the way that leadership is a journey and we are excited about sharing this leg of the journey with you.

We are excited to share with you three gifts in this book, gifts we have benefited from immensely ourselves and that continue to sharpen our own leadership.

We offer you the gift of personal interactions with some of the world's greatest leaders. We have had the chance to spend time with some amazing leaders and we draw on those experiences in this book. Leaders like Truett Cathey, the founder of Chick-fil-A. Ken Blanchard, the famous author and speaker. Frances Hesselbein, leader of the Drucker Institute. Steve Reinemund, the former head of Pepsi and now an esteemed business school dean. British business guru, Charles Handy. Pete Coors, of Molson-Coors Brewing Company. And Tom Cousins, the legendary business executive who led perhaps the most remarkable transformation of an at-risk community in American history. In fact, the first couple of chapters of this book will dig deep into that story, the Miracle at East Lake.

But this is not just about well-known people and grandiose stories of change. We will also share the gift that we've been given as we interact with ordinary people. Middle managers with government jobs. Pastors of small churches. Executives in corporate America. Volunteers in non-profit organizations. What we have learned from them has changed our view of the world.

We offer you the gift of many practical tools that you can begin to use today— right now! These tools will immediately improve your leadership skills.

We have one more gift we would like to offer you—the gift of a Triangle that has shaped and reshaped our understanding of leadership.

At the core of the Leadership Triangle is the belief that different kinds of leadership challenges call for different types of *Leadership Options*—choices the leader can make. We are passionate about helping you identify what sort of challenges you as a leader are facing and then choosing the right Option to deal with them. We believe that if you understand and, more important, act within this framework then your effectiveness as a leader will be multiplied many times.

We are honored that you have chosen to spend this time with us, reading our book and running this leg of the leadership journey along with us. Here's to our growth and effectiveness as leaders! Let us introduce you to one of the most compelling leadership stories we've ever encountered. Are you ready to dig in?

Section One
Leadership has Three Options

Chapter One
A Letter and A Phone Call

Not Your Average Phone Call

I turned up the volume for the third time, trying to absorb what I was watching. I was in a hotel room, somewhere on a client trip, probably in Seattle, when I saw Tom. An old family friend. On late night TV. Why was Tom on TV?

I remember swimming in his pool when I was four years old. Seeing him at dinner last summer in the mountains. He had never been one for the limelight, but here he was on national TV.

That same night, in a different city, Warren turned on the same news segment. We were miles apart. Tom was in Atlanta. Warren was in Omaha. And I think I was in Seattle. But that news segment crossed general boundaries and time zones in ways that had far-reaching implications.

I've never met Warren and doubt that I ever will. But Tom and Warren had known each other for many years and considered each other allies and even friends. But Warren had never heard about a project in Atlanta that Tom was finishing. A project that very few people believed in. A project designed to transform one of the worst neighborhoods in the city, a place the locals called "Little Vietnam." And here was Tom, on national TV, talking about that project. I turned up the volume once more, fully engaged even though my body said it was 2:00 a.m.

The neighborhood was called East Lake. It had a storied past, including the distinction of being the location of the golf course called home by the legendary golfer Bobby Jones. It was a resort where Atlanta's well-heeled had socialized, cut business deals, and sipped single malt Scotch at the nineteenth hole.

But that was decades ago. A public housing project—East Lake Meadows had been erected in East Lake decades later. Over the years, the project had become known for its violent crime and drug culture. By the mid-1990s, if you had the courage to take a drive through the littered streets of East Lake Meadows, you would see the tawdriest of landscapes.

The grassless yards scattered with debris. The ramshackle houses, most with boarded windows and sagging porches—they all had the unmistakable look and smell of decay.

Some residents never came out of their homes, terrified of the streets. Other residents, sullen of expression and with eyes forlorn of light, roamed the streets like vagabond kings. You would see men exchanging crumpled wads of cash for dime bags, out in broad daylight.

Tom had mastered the facts about East Lake Meadows— facts that painted an almost inconceivable portrait of pain and hopelessness. A sky high crime rate, possibly Georgia's highest. A mortality rate that sounded like an impoverished African nation. An impossibly high rate of births to unwed teenage mothers. Almost endemic illiteracy.

But Tom was a stubborn man—all of his friends said so. He was determined that this sort of place should not exist in his city, not in Atlanta. And he was determined that he was going to be a part of turning it around. He knew that if the transformation were to happen it would take way more than one man's determined efforts. It would take a team—a tough, talented, devoted team. A stubborn team.

He started dreaming dreams, rattling cages and enlisting supporters and leaders. He started describing his dreams and meeting with almost uniform disbelief and derision.

"East Lake Meadows?!" they would say. "The worst place in the country? All you will be doing is throwing good money after bad and wasting your time in the bargain. Forget it, Tom. It can't be done."

He knew they had a point or two. The problems in East Lake Meadows were not simple ones; they were ones that would require change at the most fundamental level. Where would such an effort even start? With crime reduction, education, drug treatment, or with economic revitalization? How many people— politicians and Tenants Association leaders, government bureaucrats, real estate developers looking to turn a buck— would have to work together for a common purpose? This was going to be a monumental challenge.

Fifteen years after the project started, but only a few days after the TV show aired on CNBC, Tom got Warren's letter. It came from halfway across the country and it was simple. "I saw a television program on what you are doing there in Atlanta. I think it just might work in other places. If you need anything, I have access to resources. Just call me and let me know."

So Tom did call, even before putting the letter down. "Warren," he said, "thanks for your letter. I would like your help. I don't need your money for East Lake. But I would like your help in replicating this model in other cities."

That ten minute television segment started us down the path of thinking about the Leadership Triangle. It formed a backdrop for how we, at TAG Consulting, think about leadership. It was part of what drew Ken Tucker to join our consulting practice and to co-author this book with me.

And that ten minute television segment was the impetus for Warren Buffett to join Tom Cousins in trying to change the world.

Transformation at East Lake Meadows

When it comes to leadership we can all agree on one thing: it is not easy!

The world moves at a screamingly fast pace, demanding lightning fast response times and decisions made on the fly. A fundamentally changing economy means that long taken-for-granted ground rules are out the window and the "new normal" isn't always clear. Social media has transformed the way organizations of all kinds communicate with their constituencies and customers. The traditional rules governing production and distribution of goods and services have given way to a new order where consumers are also producers.

This complexity affects organizations of all types—in the for-profit, not-for-profit, and public sectors. For-profits must compete with fast-rising economies in other parts of the world and navigate industries which seem to change overnight. Not-for-profits must contend with often aging donor bases and increased competition for dollars from the public and private sectors. And political pundits wonder openly if the United States is even governable anymore.

And we have to lead in the middle of all this complexity! If you have been leading a group for any length of time we bet you have found that time-tested methods of leadership don't seem to be working as well as they used to.

The most pressing leadership question of the moment is not just about profits or growth or shareholder value or market share. It is: "What does it mean to lead in such a way that my team or organization can adapt, compete, and thrive at levels beyond the surface?" This is the case whether you are leading a business, a department, a volunteer board, or a church committee.

This is the challenge that Tom Cousins and his team faced at East Lake Meadows in Atlanta.

East Lake had once been legacy ground for Bobby Jones, regarded as one of the greatest and unquestionably the most important golfer of all time. Jones won championship after championship without relinquishing his amateur status, foregoing paychecks for a pure love of the game. He battled a debilitating disease that would have robbed the spirits of many a lesser man. He founded the legendary Augusta National Golf Club where every spring the most prestigious professional tournament in America, the Masters, is played.

So it makes sense that the place where Bobby Jones played his first and last round would be hallowed ground for lovers of the game everywhere. And it made it all the more sad when this site, the East Lake Country Club in Atlanta, Georgia, had fallen into disrepair in the 1970s. Once lush fairways were patchy and browning. Greens were worn and diseased. Formerly lush tee boxes offered bare spots that promised to snap tees in two.

But the golf course was the least of the East Lake area's problems. Once a haven for the well-heeled of Atlanta to socialize, golf, consummate business deals, and sip cocktails, a half century of wear and tear and the city's growth in other directions meant that East Lake had lost its luster by the 1960s. And then came the fateful decision to build a public housing project in East Lake on the site of the Number Two golf course.

East Lake Meadows was in trouble from the start. Its 650 units were home to some of the most desperately poor residents in the United States. Poverty led to hopelessness, which led to a desire to escape, which led to drugs and alcohol, which led to crime, which led to cycles of gruesome violence.

Residents kept their blinds drawn even during the daytime. Every neighbor had a story of seeing a mugging or a shooting or a robbery. Atlantans called the East Lake area "Little Vietnam" and stayed away in droves. Police simply called East Lake Meadows a "war zone."

By 1995, East Lake Meadows was one of the poorest, most violent communities in the nation. The crime rate was eighteen times the national average. The employment rate (not the UNemployment rate, mind you) was at 14 percent. The average age of a grandmother in East Lake Meadows was thirty-two. That's right. Thirty-two.

East Lake Meadows was a desperately poor, desperately despised area, forgotten by its city, largely ignored by its city's leaders. A place of problems both systemic and individual. A place without hope. Until a wealthy sixty-something developer with a passion for golf picked up the *New York Times* one day.

The NYT article pointed out that the vast majority of inmates in New York's state prison system were from a small handful of neighborhoods—no more than eight. Cousins told us that he reasoned the same must be true in Georgia. So he asked Atlanta's chief of police. "Sure, Tom, everyone knows that," said the Chief. Only, in Georgia, 75 percent of the prison population comes out of maybe five neighborhoods in Atlanta alone. And most of those come out of ONE neighborhood—East Lake. "Little Vietnam. One of the worst places in the world."

Cousins had heard of East Lake Meadows but he decided to ask around. What he found stunned him. But the true day of reckoning was when he braved a field trip to the project itself. "I could not believe this was a place in America," he told us later, shaking his head.

When he began talking about his hopes to transform the area, his friends and other Atlanta leaders began shaking *their* heads. The problems are too deep and severe, he was told. That would be throwing good money after bad, they said. We'd be better off to tear the place down and start over or maybe just wall the whole neighborhood off, some argued. Most daunting of all, the people living in the community will never trust you, some said convincingly.

But Cousins was tenacious by nature and gripped by a growing vision to break the cycle of poverty and despair in East Lake Meadows. And golf—of all games, the game of the wealthy elite—provided him an entry point.

Cousins loved the game of golf and was a very good player. Once, while playing with the legendary pro golfer Jack Nicklaus in a Pro-Am event, Cousins was actually leading Nicklaus as they prepared to tee off on the seventeenth hole. Nicklaus looked at

A Fast Rise To The Top

Tom Cousins, entrepreneur and successful businessn
moved to Atlanta in 1954. His first job was respectable but ha
indicative of the career that was to come. He parlayed that in
job with a company that manufactured kits for homebuilders i
a home building company of his own. By the early 1960s, Cous
was the largest homebuilder in the state of Georgia. In the m
1960s he got into commercial and office development and l
success grew exponentially.

Cousins' résumé is nothing short of stunning. This onetim
pre-med student who nearly fainted the first time he witnesse
a surgical procedure was largely responsible for transformin
downtown Atlanta in the 1980s. He developed the CNN Center,
191 Peachtree Tower, and built the largest skyscraper in the nation
outside of Chicago and New York City. He organized and chaired
Atlanta's Billy Graham Crusade. Cousins donated the land for the
Georgia World Congress Center. He brought pro basketball (the
Atlanta Hawks) and major league hockey (the Atlanta Flames,
now the Calgary Flames) to the city. When his basketball team
needed a larger arena, he built the Omni which at the time was a
state of the art sports complex.

An innately humble man, Cousins enjoyed social prestige
political influence, and immense wealth. He had plenty of time t
play his beloved game of golf, along with a passionate desire t
help others. Life was good and his had been well lived. But the
one day he picked up the *New York Times* and began the journe
that would lead him to the greatest challenge of his career—bein
part of the team that would lead the transformation of East Lal
Meadows.

Cousins and said, "Tom, have you ever considered joining us on the professional tour?"Cousins promptly hit his next shot, sending the ball directly into a lake. Later, Cousins asked Nicklaus if the golfer had been trying to get in his head and Nicklaus just smiled.

But beyond playing and enjoying the game himself, Cousins saw that golf could be leveraged for a bigger purpose. So he set his sights on the East Lake Club.

Threadbare and unable to attract golfers because of the neighboring war zone, East Lake Golf Club was struggling. Disputes between the private partners who owned the course had ended up in court and the judge had ordered them to sell the Club. Tom Cousins paid the price himself—twenty-five million dollars—and hatched an ingenious plan.

If he could convince one hundred new corporate members to sign up for the club, paying an initiation fee of $50,000 and making a suggested donation of $200,000 to the East Lake Foundation he would leverage the resources of the Cousins Family Foundation to renovate the golf club. Of the first one hundred, $200,000 donations half would go to support the community programs of the East Lake Foundation and half was paid to the Cousins Family Foundation to offset the renovation and other costs. After that, all of the remaining $200,000 and any future profits from the East Lake Golf Club would be returned to the East Lake Foundation (this continues today and, in addition, all profits from the PGA TOUR Championship event held at the club go to the foundation). A natural salesman and a deeply convincing man, Cousins got the members he needed. But the climb up the mountain had just begun. Tom Cousins would need all the resources of his vast experience, network of contacts, and sustaining Christian faith to make it to the top.

For one thing, Cousins' vision was not just about East Lake. From the outset, he envisioned that what happened in East Lake would point the way to a transferable model which could be taken to similar communities across the nation.

Cousins faced a task that would have intimidated a lesser leader. He had come to the end of his ability—by himself—to create change. Now, he had to form a series of alliances with individuals and groups who usually viewed their interests and values as in conflict. He had to convince them to cast aside personal agendas, deep-seated distrust, and even personal security to work together to accomplish a seemingly impossible task. The change East Lake Meadows needed was not incremental, but rather transformational. A whole new community was to be created, shaped by people behaving in ways very unusual for them.

First would be the residents themselves. Battered by crime, poverty, disease, and shattered families, the good-hearted residents of East Lake Meadows would have to believe—and act on the belief—that this plan initiated by outsiders would work and would be in their best interests. Most dramatically, they would have to move out of their homes for a time so that the community could be rebuilt, having only Tom Cousins' word for a guarantee that they would be welcomed back.

Things did not go well initially. A local leader told Eva Davis, the formidable head of the neighborhood association, that Cousins was "sneaky" and should bear watching. Eva Davis had stymied former President Jimmy Carter not too long ago. She wasn't afraid of a real estate developer. Not one to be fooled easily, Eva refused to cooperate until she had reason to trust.

But even if Cousins could convince the residents of East Lake Meadows to go along, he still had to run a gamut. He would have to create a public-private partnership like Atlanta had never seen. Businesses and financial institutions would have to inject large amounts of capital into a never-before-proven idea. Political leaders would have to cooperate with housing and zoning variances and do the thing that politicians loathe to do—spend political capital.

This is a theme that we come back to again and again in the East Lake story—no one person could make the change needed alone. People were going to have to be persuaded to behave in surprising ways, ways that might at first appear to go against their self-interest.

Behaving In Unpredictable Ways

That was just the thing, Cousins soon realized. People were going to have to do things that were the precise opposite of what they would normally be inclined to do. Residents who trusted no one would have to trust strangers. Individuals with cash who normally required a great return on investment and lots of guarantees would have to risk it all. And political leaders skilled at minimizing risk, and playing the angles in their own favor would have to act selflessly. So Tom Cousins began to paint a vision and woo a city. In so doing, he created a masterpiece of leadership that is a guiding narrative of *The Leadership Triangle.*

He had always believed in bringing people together to accomplish common goals. Once, in the early 1960s Cousins had led an initiative to bring African-American and white leaders together. At one meeting, Cousins was seated across from Dr. Martin Luther King, Jr. At one point during the meeting King, Jr., who was just becoming prominent, turned to Cousins and said, "What do you think of me?" Cousins smiled and replied, "I hear you are a rabble rouser and a law breaker!" King, Jr. laughed and said, "Yes, that's right, but I am willing to pay the price." So was Tom Cousins.

Cousins and his team were forced to operate at an extraordinarily high level to meet such a wide range of challenges. He had to navigate very specific and complex tactical obstacles that required great expertise and skill. He had to understand the external environment and formulate a strategy that would succeed in the face of opposition and long odds. He had to create alignment among groups that at times saw themselves in fundamental opposition to one another.

And, most challenging of all, the team had to transform values, which involved the essential and often agonizing work of exposing the existing values of all the involved parties—values that were often in conflict.

Those are the things that truly transformational leaders do. And, we will see, these are the things that **you** can do whether you are a businessperson, head of a not-for-profit or a volunteer organization, or leader of a church. The challenges that faced East Lake and Tom Cousins were unique—as are yours—but the principles of the Leadership Triangle which he practiced are universal.

So, what was the vision Cousins painted as he sought to persuade across tables in corporate boardrooms, restaurants fancy and plain, the mansions in Buckhead and the broken down homes of East Lake Meadows?

A New Foundation, A New Dream

In Tom Cousins' imagination East Lake Meadows would be a model community, full of hard-working, law-abiding citizens who looked out for one another. The residents would be a testament to the belief—the fact—that predictable cycles of poverty, crime and despair are not inevitable.

To help make the vision a reality, Cousins plowed his own money into a new organization—the East Lake Foundation—designed to provide common ground to the diverse parties who were necessary to the project. The Foundation's goal was to "help transform the East Lake neighborhood and create new opportunities for the families that live there." Community "redevelopment" was a common phrase in 1995. The East Lake vision was more about community re-creation.

The project would require participation—to greater and lesser degrees—from a wide range of players. There were public partners (the Atlanta Housing Authority, the Atlanta Public Schools, and a critical grant from the U.S. government), private partners (Emory University, Oglethorpe University, the Publix grocery store chain, the YMCA) and financial partners (SunTrust and Wells Fargo banks). At the outset, in the middle, and towards the end of the project, each of these entities would play a role. Most important of all, there were the residential partners in East Lake Meadows itself.

And there were individual leaders whom Cousins recruited to the cause— successful men and women from academia, the marketplace, the legal profession—all of whom subordinated their egos and risked their reputations to enlist against daunting odds. People like Renee Glover, Madelyn Adams, Charlie Harrison, Don Edwards, Lillian and Greg Giornelli, Carol Naughton, Chuck

Knapp, and the eventual mayor of Atlanta, Shirley Franklin. You will meet many of them in this book.

The once skeptical Eva Davis began to spend time with Cousins and his family and, in her own words, "came to love them." Traditional economic and racial boundaries began to dissolve as she saw that he really cared about her neighborhood and its people and, significantly, had the power and influence to actually bring change. Eva Davis began to leverage her influence to do the unthinkable—persuade her neighbors to move into temporary housing so that the dilapidated buildings of East Lake Meadows could be transformed into the Villages of East Lake. And, slowly, the transformation began to happen.

In this book, we will share many stories that illustrate how Tom Cousins, his colleagues, and many other leaders exemplified the principles of the Leadership Triangle. But, for now, let's just capture a snapshot view of East Lake in 2011.

East Lake Meadows is now the Villages of East Lake, with 542 mixed income housing units. Half of the units are reserved for families who receive public assistance, and nearly all of those families have heads of household who are either working or receiving job training. The other half of the units are reserved for middle income families.

The broader East Lake Community includes the Charles R. Drew Charter School, Atlanta's first charter school which has 800 students in pre-kindergarten through eighth grade. In 2010 at Drew, 96 percent of the students met or exceeded state requirements for reading and 91 percent did so for math.

There is Sheltering Arms Early Education and Family Center, providing care for kids from birth to kindergarten. There is a pristine East Lake Family YMCA and a well-stocked Publix grocery store.

Violent crime is down a staggering 95 percent. The percentage of residents on welfare has declined from 58 percent to 5 percent. The employment rate for those receiving public assistance has skyrocketed from 14 to 71 percent.

A Crucial Link

And there is golf. The prestigious PGA TOUR Championship is held on the Rees Jones-redesigned East Lake Golf Club, but that is not the most important "golf" thing.

East Lake is the home to the "First Tee of East Lake program," a rapidly expanding effort to leverage the beauty of the game of golf to mentor and shape at- risk youngsters. Sponsored by the World Foundation of Golf, First Tee uses the lessons of golf to teach participants "life-affirming" values such as honesty, integrity, commitment, and excellence.

Those values are part of the reason Tom Cousins loves golf so much. He sees in the game a unique emphasis on personal accountability and moral character, talents or traits that dovetail with his deep Christian faith and the way he has lived his life. In East Lake golf, the most "elite" of games, is helping at-risk kids learn values and patterns of behavior which will help them navigate the world outside the boundaries of East Lake.

East Lake, remember, is where the world's most important golfer—Bobby Jones—played his first and last rounds. It is a source of inspiration to Tom Cousins and to many others that East

Lake today could be fostering other golfers who will play and live with excellence.

Beyond the Statistics, Stories

As we begin our journey of understanding the Leadership Triangle and how its principles can shape the way you lead in your own setting, we will look back to the East Lake story a few more times. We hope you will find it as encouraging and inspiring as we do. It is a story that offers instruction, for sure. But more important, it offers hope of transformation.

Perhaps Eva Davis puts it best…

"We tore down hell and replaced it with heaven!"

Chapter Two
Three Leadership Options

You've heard this said before: "When the only tool in your toolbox is a hammer, everything looks like a nail." The truth behind the cliché applies not just to carpentry, but to leadership as well. A classic leadership pitfall is to find an approach to problem-solving that worked in the past and use it every time. Automatically. For years. And decades. And then wonder why it doesn't work anymore.

For example, much of the leadership literature of the last twenty years has emphasized the importance of "vision." Paint a clear and compelling picture of the future, you are told, and you cannot fail as a leader. The most lionized leaders are those who took the reins of dysfunctional and aimless organizations, crafted and articulated a clear vision of the future, and reached the heights of success. We have gotten good at crafting compelling narratives of a preferred future and almost no one questions the value of having a vision shared by those throughout the organization.

But what happens when you're still stuck?

As consultants, we are called to serve many organizations that have a great vision for the future. Their leaders have worked long and hard to imagine the future and to paint a word picture that draws others in and keeps them motivated. These leaders have wielded the hammer of vision with skill and passion. But something is still missing. What could it be?

Solving the Wrong Problem
If you're not making any progress in solving the problem you're facing, you are probably trying to solve the wrong problem.

Problems are always subject to interpretation. Assume that the current interpretation is probably wrong. Look at the issue from a different perspective. Try revisiting the origin of the issue: "This issue would not be a problem if...."

Recently, we met with former mortgage banker Becky Walker, now the Executive Director for Treehouse Youth (www.treehouseyouth.org), a Minneapolis-based non-profit. Treehouse provides programs, counseling, and events to teens that are living in dysfunctional settings. Surprisingly, many of these teens are not the prototypical inner city kids. Many of them come from suburbia. Treehouse operates on a small budget of $3 million, has a star-studded board of directors (including Gregg Steinhafel, Chairman and CEO of Target Corporation), and recently hosted a gala that featured Super Bowl-winning coach Tony Dungy and country music star Carrie Underwood.

Over 1,400 teens participated in their programs between April 2007 and May 2008. The teens come from all kinds of backgrounds, but have one thing in common: they have been unloved by parents and teachers. In fact, when Fred Peterson founded the organization in 1984, he started by asking teachers to give him a list of all the kids that they wish would not come to school. These kids are struggling with dangers presented by the Internet, abuse at home, drugs, unwanted pregnancies, and more.

Treehouse provides trained counselors and quality programming to give them resources to cope with the challenges of daily living. The results have been nothing short of astounding:

- Most of the participants now have an adult in their lives whom they trust

- Many indicate that they are now equipped to deal with the bad things in their lives

- A significant number of teens feel like their lives are now under control

- More than half have either decreased or eliminated all risky behaviors

For many years, Treehouse focused exclusively on the western suburbs in Minneapolis. They owned their own facilities. But in recent years, they sold their facilities and found that they could leverage existing properties, such as empty churches, and expand their reach. Their vision is grand—to plant a Treehouse in every community in the U.S.

As we talked with Becky, it occurred to us that "vision is not the problem." So what was the problem? Becky admitted to struggling with questions like these:

- How do we get our board of directors to agree on the best strategy? Many of them have never worked in a non-profit environment.

- How do we raise financial support, especially in this economy? I can't raise capital like I did in the mortgage banking industry.

- Do we have the right staffing? I can't be in two places at once.

- How do we change the culture from being so rigid to becoming more supportive and empowering?

- How do we raise awareness, leverage the media, and capitalize on marketing opportunities?

Some of these struggles are organizational, but others are personal and unique to Becky. As a former mortgage banker, she is finding that she is being called upon to learn new skills, ask different questions, and try different strategies in the non-profit context. She needs more than one Leadership Option!

Think again of Tom Cousins. To be sure, he had a passionate vision for East Lake Meadows: a safe, thriving community where residents partnered with each other and outside agencies to break the cycle of poverty and despair. But if vision had been the only tool in his leadership toolbox, the East Lake transformation would never have gotten off the ground. The challenges he faced went way beyond painting a picture of the future. He had to take into account a brutal past, a dangerous present, mistrust, broken relationships, and systemic sickness.

Leadership is not just an attribute. Leadership is also when you and your team identify a problem and know that you must choose from an array of options to tackle that problem. A skillful leader chooses the right *option* which results in exponential success.

But when the leader chooses the wrong option, then the solution can become part of the problem itself. This is the unseen iceberg right underneath the waterline in the leadership challenge. Our commitment is to help you understand what sorts of problems you are facing so that you can choose the right option.

To get at that, this chapter will offer an overview of the three Leadership Options—the Leadership Triangle. And the rest of the book will describe how you can use the Triangle to understand the kinds of problems your organization is facing so that you will be in the optimum position to choose the best option.

In our years as consultants, we have identified three primary types of leadership challenges, represented by the three sides of the Triangle. Each challenge requires a different mode of leadership behavior in response, a different "option." Most leaders fail to identify the type of problem, and therefore fall back on their preferred, or default, option. The art of leadership is in knowing what sort of problem you are facing and what leadership option is required to tackle it. Each problem requires a different set of skills, language, questions, and styles of interaction.

Let's pause to give credit where credit is due. We have been influenced by the work of Richard Chait, who, in his writings about non-profit boards of directors, identifies three types of work that boards must do to be effective. Noting that most boards limit their work to budgets and by-laws (the fiduciary work), he challenges boards of directors to recognize that there is also "strategic" work and "generative" work to do. While Chait focuses on board governance, his concepts helped us clarify what we have long seen in our clients, effective leadership must work in multiple modalities. You need more than one tool in your toolbox!

First, let's insure that we understand each kind of leadership challenge by exploring descriptors for each side of the Triangle.

Tactical Challenges

Tactical issues can also be called "operational," "technical," or "fiduciary." Tactical challenges are the daily bread of the operations-oriented manager.

Tactical issues are solved by expertise. If the roof leaks, you call a roofer. If your driveway is covered with snow, you hire the neighbor's teenage kid who has a shovel. If your hard drive crashes, you call the Geek Squad. An astute leader faces tactical problems by identifying the right expert who offers the right solution and empowering them to solve the problem.

A Tactical Scenario

An association's communications administrator is fielding complaints from members that communication between staff and members is slow and unreliable. The administrator investigates and finds that the staff is using old, bulky computers with outdated hardware and software. So he calls an information technology professional who comes in, evaluates the situation, and makes a series of recommendations to the administrator. The administrator finds money within the budget, purchases new hardware and software and makes sure the staff is well-trained. A tactical problem is solved by a tactical solution.

If only all such problems were so simple. But one of the biggest mistakes we see leaders make is to apply simple tactical solutions to problems that are not tactical in nature.

Various tactical solutions had been attempted at East Lake. Welfare is but one example. Tom Cousins told us about a seventh grade teacher who came to him with the story of a twelve-year-old girl. This promising young student informed her teacher that she wouldn't be coming back the following year. When asked why, she explained that her mom wanted her to have a baby. If they had another dependent in the family, they would receive more welfare assistance. So this twelve-year-old was virtually giving up any possibility of education and a future to receive a few dollars per month. Cousins virtually wept as he told us this story—an example of how a well-intentioned tactical solution had unintentionally created a new set of problems.

We once worked with a manager who was having a bad day. He was leading a meeting and several of the employees present were chattering, laughing and in general ignoring the manager. After the meeting he called them into his office and reamed them out.

After he had cooled down overnight he thought better of his actions. So he purchased a single rose for each employee whom he had scolded and placed it on their desks as a way of apologizing. A nice gesture which surely fixed the problem, right? Wrong.

In fact, the roses became a negative symbol in the office, a powerful indicator of one-upsmanship. Employees without a rose felt left out and employees with the rose viewed the flower as a token of their power over the manager and their enhanced place in the office hierarchy. What went wrong?

The manager had misunderstood the nature of the problem. He thought the issue was employees being rude during a meeting and his own temper tantrum. Simple, tactical stuff requiring a simple tactical solution– a few bucks and some flowers.

When in fact, the problem was a transformational one (more on this in a moment) – a workplace that was hostile and a culture characterized by disrespect. The roses actually made the situation worse by deepening division and eroding trust. A well-intentioned manager had misunderstood the problem and chosen the wrong solution, which contributed to the problem. This is why it is so important for you to understand ALL sides of the Triangle before choosing an option.

Strategic Challenges

Strategic challenges have to do with responding to the world outside your organization. These challenges are not necessarily problems to be solved, but challenges you can anticipate. Strategy has to do with surveying the environment outside your department or organization and deciding how best your team can adapt to external opportunities and obstacles.

In the face of strategic challenges, tactical effectiveness is not enough. Anyone can operate effectively and still go out of business, fail in a charitable fund-raising endeavor, or coach a losing team. Strategy is when you choose a **unique value proposition** through a series of activities that become rooted in your system. Essentially, strategy is what differentiates your organization from any other.

A business finds the core needs of its customers changing and so must decide on new lines of products and services. A church sees its neighborhood's demographics changing rapidly and must decide how to respond with programs and worship services. A non-profit sees its core mission taken over by a new local government program and must decide what new human need to meet.

When you are using the Strategic Option, you are observing challenges that are rooted in the future. These challenges are about transitioning from one generation to the next, or one era to the next. Such challenges require more than a tactical fix. Strategic challenges require you to use strategic leadership– the art of leveraging strengths in order to minimize weaknesses and capitalize on opportunities.

A Strategic Scenario

Suppose you are a board member in this scenario: A highly regarded not-for-profit focuses its mission on arts education in schools in lower income neighborhoods which must often forgo any sort of arts curriculum. The not-for-profit depends on the generosity of foundations and individuals in the community and an annual grant from the local arts and sciences council.

Then an economic downturn ravages the city in which the not-for-profit is based. Unemployment skyrockets as the major industries in the community merge or fold. A nationwide recession leads to a declining pool of charitable resources.

At its semi-annual board meeting, you hear the shell-shocked Executive Director describe a 20 percent decline in contributions to the organization over the past year and the bad news that the arts and science council grant will be trimmed in half in the coming year. How do you respond? Try harder? Fire the Executive Director? Hire a different fund raising company? Probably not. As a board member, you are more likely to approach this from the Strategic Option by asking a series of strategic questions:

- Since we can't maintain our present level of service, what should we offer or not offer from our current menu?

- Is arts education a pressing issue in our hurting community and, if not, what other needs should we meet?

- What sorts of alternative programs could we offer that might cost less money?

- How do we maintain quality if we are forced to reduce personnel?

- We focus on five areas now; should we reduce that focus to one or two to ride out this downturn?

- What needs in our constituency are we best equipped to meet at the present time?

Strategic challenges require a different, and in some ways more sophisticated, set of skills than tactical problems. But strategic acumen does not cover every type of leadership challenge. Often, when strategic direction is established, the result is that a whole different set of issues surface—issues related to values, behaviors, and attitudes. It is this most complex type of challenge that is illustrated by the third side of the Leadership Triangle.

Transformational Challenges

Transformational problems are the truly vital challenges, the ones which relate to values, behaviors, and attitudes. Transformational problems are often rooted in the system and are not usually visible to the naked eye. These are the ones that keep you up at night, the ones that tempt you to think, "We'll never be able to solve this one!"

The essence of a transformational problem is in the concept of "competing values." In the East Lake scenario, Tom Cousins had to balance the competing values of corporations and financial institutions (making investments which would result in profit to their shareholders), political leaders (minimizing political risk to insure re-election) and the residents of East Lake themselves (maintaining a place to live and some measure of personal security).

Your real work of leadership will be done on the transformational level as you accept and even provoke conflict over values so that clarity can be reached and real change can be created. Sounds daunting, doesn't it?

A Transformational Scenario

One of our client churches was located in suburban St. Louis. We were called in to help with strategic planning by the new pastor.

The former pastor was the classic chaplain. Warm, compassionate and people-oriented he was brilliant over coffee in the living room and at the hospital bedside. He was beloved by his people not so much for his preaching ability or leadership skills as for his ability to make each congregant feel loved, included, and cared for and to foster a sense of community and connection among his people.

The new pastor loved people too, but his strengths were quite different than his predecessor's. This pastor's skill set was in the areas of teaching and leadership. In particular, he was a gifted visionary able to see and articulate a future for the church that was both exciting and very different from its past and present.

The church began to grow quite rapidly, fueled by an influx of young professional families.

Predictably, the church began to be polarized not long into the new pastorate. Folks who were wired to appreciate strong visionary leadership gravitated to the new pastor as a breath of fresh air. Those who had been drawn to the church under the predecessor pastor's leadership missed his people skills and ability to generate congregational warmth and belonging.

When we sat down with a group of leaders, it became clear that the problem was not one of personalities but rather of values. One group—those drawn to the old pastor—spoke of missing the family feeling of past years. "The church is not a business, it is a family," they argued. "We can't depart from that family feeling or we will become a sterile institution without a heart." The other group—resonating with the new pastor—said that the church needed to be a better-run organization if it was going to have the opportunity to impact its surrounding community in a significant way. "We can't be an inner-focused club," they argued. "We have to have a bold vision and make decisions more like a well-run business. This is how we can best carry out our spiritual mandate."

We let them argue and discuss for thirty minutes or so before intervening gently. "What if the real issue is not 'family' vs. 'business'?" we suggested. "What if what is really going on here is a very healthy conflict over the value of what 'church' is to be? What if the real answer is not an either-or 'family' vs. 'business' but something else entirely that we may not have thought of yet; 'church' vs. 'family or business.'"

They were a bit confused at first so we spent the next several hours debating over the differences between "church vs. family" and "church vs. business." A family takes care of its own, they said. A church exists for those on the outside. A business produces a profit, while a church glorifies God. Sure, a church needs to take care of people and pay bills, but it is much more significant than a business and much more outwardly focused than a family. The participants were full of energy and excitement. They were finding their way towards a new reality and way of thinking which promised to move them forward in developing a vision for the future.

A Hard Fact And The Promise of Hope

Your first job as a leader is to diagnose what sort of problem you are being faced with. Is this an issue for an expert that involves a transparent fix (Tactical)? Is it an issue that involves factors outside of the organization and requires change in leadership (Strategic)? Or is it a deeper, systemic challenge relating to competing values and beliefs (Transformational)?

The Leader's Role

Tactical—The leader is an expert. The tactical leader approaches problems with a particular knowledge base, or skill set, to solve specific problems.

Strategic—The leader is a synthesizer, identifying patterns and trends. The strategic leader sees beyond current realities.

Transformational—The leader is a facilitator. The transformational leader doesn't make decisions or establish strategic plans but, instead, facilitates a series of conversations among key stakeholders.

And your second job is to choose an appropriate option based on the nature of the problem. It sounds simple. So, why is leadership so hard? The answer lies in the nature of our default responses to leadership challenges, one of the crucial concepts of this book.

Every leader has a default response to a problem. In our experience, 90 percent of leaders default to a Tactical Option. Ten percent default to a Strategic Option. Virtually no one defaults to a Transformational Option. And this is why we are so often stuck.

It is our passion and ambition to help you get unstuck by discovering how to become skilled at using each of the options of leadership. And that is where we are going together in the remainder of our book. The following sections will each examine one side of the Leadership Triangle, focusing on the types of challenges you face as a leader and the best Option to choose for each one. Along the way, we'll tell stories and share insights from key leaders who have excelled with each Option.

Section Two of our book will help you to tackle strategic challenges, Section Three will focus on tactical challenges, and Section Four will focus on transformational challenges. It's important to note briefly why we have chosen this order.

We start with the Strategic Option because that is where the work of leadership begins—with mission, vision, and strategic choices. Once those foundational elements are in place, you can move to implementation; this is the Tactical Option. This is where practical skills and know-how come into play, where you build and release the team to accomplish the mission.

And it is at this point that many organizations get stuck. The inevitable pushback comes but they fail to identify and deal with competing values and conflict, instead relying on a Tactical approach to push the mission across the finish line. But all too often when this happens the promised solutions become the problem. It is at this moment that you as a leader must shift into the Transformational Option. Because most leadership challenges come to us in this order, we have organized our book sequentially, in turn focusing on the Strategic, Tactical, and finally Transformational Options.

In each section we will equip you with practical tools to accurately diagnose what sort of problem you are facing and to wisely choose an option. We'll discuss the role of the leader, his or her tone, the key questions to ask, how problems are to be approached, and exactly how to interact with your team depending on the type of problem you are facing.

Here we go!

Section Two
The Strategic Option

Chapter Three
Determine Your Strategy

As we interviewed people who worked with Tom Cousins during the East Lake transformation effort they consistently told us two things: "Tom saw it when no one else could see it and he never wavered in his vision," and "Tom understood all the players and he understood the context." These two strengths—tenacious vision and environmental awareness—are the essence of effective strategy.

By his own admission, Cousins' tenacity is grounded in his faith. He begins every morning by reading Scripture and his friends say that he takes Scripture very seriously. The thing that rankles him the most is when a businessperson who purports to be a Christian is guilty of unethical dealings and hypocrisy. Cousins is a man who sees the big picture. And he sees things in their proper context.

A professor of ancient texts paused in class one day and said, "Ladies and gentlemen, I want to tell you the single most important principle in determining the meaning of a text. It is not the words themselves. It is the context in which the words are presented. The principle is this: 'Context is KING.'"

The same principle holds true for the teams you lead. The context of a team and its surrounding community—or its constituency—is all-important. Before you can lead change you must understand with crystal clarity what is going on outside your four walls and, just as important, what are the implications of that context for your team.

The writer Patrick Lencioni has popularized the concept of "death by meeting," that perilous state when an organization is so focused on its internal challenges, processes and politics that it ignores the world outside, sometimes even its own customers. Our goal in this chapter is to show you how to avoid this deadly pitfall and know how to seize skillfully the Strategic Option. Most important of all, you will learn how to read with accuracy and meaning the context of your own organization. And while we cannot teach vision, we can teach you how to pay attention to trends.

A Working Definition

Strategy is a systematic method of differentiation from the competition. It is based on priority activities, performed in unique ways, reinforced by current practices, to produce a distinct result. Everything about strategy is unique. That's why United Airlines could never reproduce Southwest Airline's strategy. Nor could McDonalds ever replicate Subway's strategy. They are in similar industries, but strategy is all about differentiation. And once something becomes commonplace (like dollar menus) in a certain context, it is no longer strategic. Everything about strategy is rooted in context.

Chuck Knapp and Tom Cousins go back a long way. After a distinguished career in university teaching, a time as a high level federal government official in Washington, D.C. and a stint as executive vice-president at Tulane University, Knapp was recruited by Cousins to serve as the president of the University of Georgia. After a number of fruitful years in Athens and a foray in consulting, Knapp was recruited by Cousins once again and until March of 2011 served as Chairman of the East Lake Foundation, an umbrella organization giving leadership to the ongoing transformation in East Lake. Part of his role as chairman was to work with Purpose-Built Communities, East Lake's effort to transmit best practices and benchmarking measures to other communities who wish to see similar transformation.

But Knapp is reluctant to use the word "replication." What will work in one place won't work in others, he says. Sure, there are some overarching principles, but you have to know the ins and outs of the particular community, you have to know the key players, you have to know "where the blood has been spilled." And you have to be driven by a unique vision for your unique place. "That," says Knapp, "is where Tom Cousins excelled."

Atlanta is a historic Southern city, with continuing racial overtones from the Civil War. It is also a New South city, progressive in its culture and politics. It has a deep and strong tradition of leadership from the African-American community, especially in politics and in its religious life. It is an inland city, dependent on commerce and development. African-Americans don't always trust white people, and vice versa. In its neighborhoods, community leaders are effective power brokers, running mini-fiefdoms, paid homage by elected officials.

In Atlanta, it was essential that a historically divided city, split between races and split between the old and new, find ways to bridge gaps both historic and contemporary if change was going to take root. Not all cities are like that—in some the interests and aspirations of politicians, businesspeople, clergy, and residents converge. But not here. Any strategy had to take head on this challenge and this imperative. This is King Context.

As for the vision? "Simple," says Knapp. "You had this tour de force in Tom Cousins saying 'This can't happen in America. This can't happen here.'"

We should mention here that vision, more often than not, is a by-product of a good strategy. In the past, most leadership theorists argued that you have to start with the "end in mind." You have to have a clear vision, and the strategy tells you how to accomplish that vision. This is what you're typically taught. We want to suggest that it's the other way around. A clear strategy, born out of a keen understanding of context, will result in a compelling vision.

A Leader's Toolkit

Each one of the leadership options requires a leader to function in distinct ways.

You'll adopt a distinct role. You'll choose a specific tone. You'll always be raising a key question. You'll have to know what to do with problems. And you'll always be working on how to interact with your team. In each section of our book, we will show you which tools to choose depending on the Option you have chosen. After all, not every problem requires a nail. Which means you can't choose the same hammer every time.

A Toolkit for the Strategic Option

Role
Your role, as a leader in choosing the Strategic Option, is that of the synthesizer. Here, you have to think like a symphony conductor, who must bring music out of a diverse collection of instruments, personalities, temperaments, and life experiences.

But conductors are more than managers. You must hear the music in your head before you can lead your orchestra. And you have to hear more than the melody or the parts for trumpet or violin or timpani—you have to hear the whole thing all at once. There has to be a synthesis of sound.

We've found that the very best conductors know about a lot more than just music! They are intense students of the culture and the communities in which their orchestras are located. They pay attention to trends—they are curious people! So, it is critical for you to be a curious person as well. Use the "five why's" as a way of uncovering trends or discovering information. Never settle for a basic answer to a basic question. Ask "why" five times. Ask a question, get an answer, and ask "why." Repeat that four more times. You'll get a lot more information than if you just take the initial answer at face value. We do this with our clients, for example, to help them discover their purpose.

"Why do you exist?" To make money.

"Why do you want to make money?" To have financial security.

"Why do you want financial security?" So my kids don't have to pay for my retirement.

"Why don't you want your kids to pay for your retirement?" So they can do what they are meant to do.

"Why do you want them to do what they are meant to do?" Because that is my purpose as a dad.

You could go beyond five questions, but make this a simple practice in conversations at work, at home, and at social events.

You'll start noticing trends and themes that will help you become a strategic leader.

As you employ the Strategic Option, you will think the same way, learning to put the pieces of the puzzle together, even when they appear to come from different boxes!

In East Lake, some of the residents desired change. Others did not. The formidable Eva Davis, president of the Homeowner's Association (much more on her later) ruled with an iron fist and desired to continue in power. All of the residents would have to leave their homes temporarily. None of them wanted to do that.

But the residents of East Lake were not the only pieces of the puzzle. Cousins had to consider the Housing Authority, business interests, zoning officials, and community activists as well. If change was to come it had to be systemic—a LOT of pieces would have to be put together. His great strength was that he saw the completed picture, not just the disparate parts. A leader operating from the Strategic Option has to keep her head up and eyes moving, scanning the landscape to see how things that have fallen apart or appear unrelated can actually come together to form a whole.

Tone

When you choose the Strategic Option, you adopt the tone of a vision-caster. After all, it is only a compelling common vision that is going to—best case scenario—cause people with different priorities to give up cherished ambitions, hand over power voluntarily, and choose to compromise. It is within the strategic option that the vision must be communicated most insistently.

The vision must be clear. Using word pictures and images of a preferred future rather than business-speak, the vision must touch both heart and mind. The follower must be able to see herself in the vision described.

And it must describe clearly how it will improve the follower's life. A recent study of various diets found that most of them don't work because the vision is not compelling. Most diets offer to prolong life. Most miserable people don't want a prolonged life, they want a better life. The diets that offer a vision of more enjoyment today are the ones that are most compelling.

The football player endures the sacrifice of two-a-days in the heat of August to get to hoist a championship trophy on a crisp fall night. A businesswoman endures stereotyping and the occasional derogatory comment to advance in her career so that she can achieve a position of maximum influence to serve others. Neither happens without a vision. And as competing constituencies scratch and claw to protect pride of place, slices of the budget pie, offices with proximity to the corridors of power, and glittering images, nothing less than a clear vision which compels and fascinates will enable them to edge towards the magic of collaboration.

Key Question

When you choose the Strategic Option, you face one key question: "What's the objective?" Then you get it done.

This is Dwight D. Eisenhower as he planned the D-Day invasions in Normandy during World War II. Forced to corral egotistical (and occasionally preening) generals from different nationalities, battle ominous weather patterns, navigate unprecedented technological challenges,

> **What's The Key Question?**
>
> Strategic—What's our objective? Let's accomplish it.
>
> Tactical—What's wrong? Let's fix it.
>
> Transformational—What's the question? Let's discover it.

and carry the weight of the free world on his shoulders, Eisenhower's focus never wavered. The invasion would take place at the right time with the right coordination with a particular chronology to accomplish this specific objective.

Let's say you are leading a sales team. Your team is facing pressure from a competitor that you didn't see coming. They have you on price point (how can they realize any margin with those prices??), their marketing makes yours look tired and stale, they are recruiting some of your people, and your reputation in the industry is suffering.

You have a strategic challenge—it's in the external environment. You could choose to focus your questions in a lot of different directions: "Who let this happen?" "How did marketing/R&D/that certain vice-president not see this coming?" "How can we preserve our dwindling market share?" "Whom can I blame to save myself?" "Let's hire a new ad agency." "Let's improve our service quality." All interesting questions or suggestions; none of them are strategic. None of them are likely to lead anywhere other than incremental change at best.

Faced with a strategic challenge, your key question will be situation-specific, but it will revolve around THIS question: "What must we do to respond to this change in the environment by differentiating ourselves from our competition, or moving into an arena where there is no competition, so that we can best fulfill our mission?"

Stance Toward Problems

When you are leading from the Strategic Option, you have to choose what you are going to do with your problems. A strategic leader realizes that a new strategy is the correct response to a strategic problem. You can't just do more of the same. It is much like parenting. If yelling at your kids doesn't work, yelling louder won't work any better.

Strategic problems require new strategies. When we are confronted with a tactical problem, we simply solve it by calling in the right expert or employing tried and true techniques that have worked for us in the past. But when we have a strategic problem we need a new way to address it. A leader choosing the Strategic Option does research, explores scenarios, and considers possible outcomes before making key decisions. This is all part of strategy.

Interaction with Teammates

At every point, you have to choose how you are going to interact with your teammates. This is important no matter the option being chosen, but it is absolutely critical in the Strategic Option. A leader must always manage to be **inspiring** when leading from the Strategic Option.

As we interviewed Tom Cousins' colleagues they came back again and again to the point that he had inspired them with his vision. Make no mistake, Cousins is not the central casting version of the smooth and inspiring motivator. He is no Tony Robbins. Though certainly charming, he can be abrupt and, we are told, even abrasive. One CEO even told us he was irascible. Motivational platitudes do not drip from his lips. But he has the ability to paint a picture of what must NOT be—and then what MUST be, that over time cause others to drop their defenses, their agendas, and in some cases their careers, to enlist in the East Lake cause.

Cousins is a force of nature in terms of his personality. But it is important to note that he did not rely on his personality, or even his presence alone to inspire others. During the most heated time of the battle, Cousins and his team had to convince Eva Davis and the homeowners of East Lake Meadows to move from their homes for a time so that their dilapidated dwellings could be razed to the ground and a new East Lake built in their place, along with schools and businesses. But no one knew whether they could trust the wealthy, white developer not to sell the land, turn a tidy profit, hold his hands out palms upwards and say, "Sorry"!

So, for a period of years, the team had to attend contentious Tenants' Association meetings where they were called every name in the book, yelled at, sometimes even kicked out. Year after year, week after week, Greg Giornelli (Cousins' son-in-law, a successful lawyer, and at this time the Director of the East Lake Foundation) and others made the dangerous trek to East Lake to take the abuse from disillusioned and frightened residents not used to trusting anybody.

One time, things got so bad that Giornelli called Cousins and said "It's over. We're licked." But he kept going back. And back. And against all odds they eventually won the trust of the residents.

Surely, Giornelli and those who went with him are tenacious folks. But behind the tenacity was an inspirational vision—communicated by a visionary who never wavered. The East Lake transformation was a monumental challenge that could not have been accomplished without the elemental motivation of a compelling vision promising an ultimate payoff. Cousins had to take different people having different experiences with different life stories holding very different ideas and bring it together into a connected whole.

A Word About Operations

Leaders who operate readily within the Tactical Option often are skilled at operational effectiveness. And such leaders often have a tendency to believe that operational effectiveness can conquer all. But here is a hard fact we have seen all too many times—you can be a beast when it comes to execution and still go out of business.

In the late 1990s Bill Fields was a much-vaunted figure in American business. The former Wal-Mart president got it just right when he said, "When the rate of external change exceeds the rate of internal change, disaster is imminent."

It's a piece of advice that the Blockbuster video rental enterprise could have used. Long dominant in the VHS rental business, for a while it appeared that Blockbuster was invulnerable. But in the last decade of the twentieth century, consumers began changing how they viewed movies in the home. First, DVDs replaced VHS. Blockbuster was slow to adapt. Then came the Internet and while Blockbuster did forge a partnership with AOL and DirectTV, the effort was halfhearted. Eventually, Blockbuster began offering online rentals and rentals through retail kiosks but only after Netflix and Red Box had beaten them to it and carved out market share.

Eventually and inevitably, Blockbuster filed for bankruptcy in September of 2010. The external environment changed at a rapid pace and while Blockbuster maintained stellar operations it was unable to create a new strategy in the digital marketplace.

Ironically, Bill Fields was Blockbuster's chief for a while in the late 1990s. Even though he understood the importance of change he didn't fully see the digital future coming.

It is essential that we get the future right. And it is to that challenge we turn next.

Chapter Four
Define Your Vision

Wayne Gretzky is universally regarded as the greatest ice hockey player of all time. Even his nickname indicates such—"The Great One." When he retired he held forty regular season records, fifteen playoff records and six All Star game records. Commentators often noted that he appeared to be playing a different, higher level game than his competitors on the ice.

Gretzky was once asked about the source of his greatness. "I suppose," he said "that a good hockey player goes to where the puck is. A great hockey player goes to where the puck is going to be." What separates great from good is the ability to anticipate the future and act decisively.

That's true not just for hockey, but also for leadership. A key part of leading from the Strategic Option is your ability to sense changes in the cultural, industrial, and competitive landscapes and to envision the future at the end of all the change. As a strategic leader, you need to envision the future and shape your team around the picture you see.

That's why Bill Gates was able to envision a personal computer in every home by the year 2000 way back in the 1970s. And why a leader of a long-gone Microsoft competitor, Digital Equipment Corporation, scratched his head in 1979 and said, "I can't understand why anyone would want a computer in their home."

It's why Jeff Bezos of Amazon.com was able to envision consumers buying books (and now thousands of other items!) online while brick and mortar bookshops like Barnes and Noble and Borders could not envision a day when readers would purchase their books without touching them first.

And it is how Netflix was able to envision movie buffs being excited to receive rental DVDs in their mailbox or streamed to their computers or Wii game consoles while Blockbuster and Hollywood Video assumed customers would always be willing to get out of the house and drive to their retail outlets.

Let's be honest—Bill Gates is a once in a generation visionary. For some, "the vision thing" is innate. But the good news is that the ability to envision the future and act accordingly is something *you* can learn!

Seeing The Future For What It Is

Innate visionaries often feel change in their gut and only later are able to explain what they saw coming. The rest of us need tools. One such tool is distinguishing between manageable, incremental change and truly epochal change that requires a transformed view of the future. Recognizing fundamental change for what it is, is a crucial skill for the leader operating in the Strategic Option.

Andy Grove is the legendary former Chairman and CEO of the Intel Corporation. During his tenure, Intel realized a 4,500 percent increase in market capitalization (that's right, TWO zeros) which made Intel at the time the world's most valuable company. Grove is a skilled manager, to be sure, but his great contribution was to reinvent Intel—totally transforming the company from a memory chip manufacturer to the market leader in micro-processing. He had the vision to see the change in computing hardware and the guts to re-make his company.

Grove distinguishes between garden variety change and the kind of change that represents a fundamental change in the competitive environment, what he calls Strategic Inflection Points. They are the points of no return, where the future is altered and organizations must change or die.

A Strategic Inflection Point is the breakup of the Bell System in telecommunications in 1984, forever changing the competitive landscape, segmenting the market, and opening the market to hundreds of new companies. It is when the mom and pop hardware store sees Wal-Mart breaking ground on a new super store a half a mile away. It is when personal computing can be downsized from the mainframe to the desktop. It is when traditional publishers try to sell their goods in a world where consumers can produce and distribute their own content.

See the Inflection Point coming and you can adapt your business to seize new opportunities. Miss it and you are headed for a new career path in some other industry.

Grove offers two key tips for seeing a Strategic Inflection Point for what it is.

First is the "silver bullet test." This is when your main competitor is suddenly different than it has been. If you have only one bullet in your gun, who would you "shoot?" If the answer is different than it has always been, you may be staring at a Strategic Inflection Point.

Second is when people you have worked with for a long time suddenly begin talking "gibberish," apparently consumed with other priorities, challenges, and threats than in the past. "This is a sign," says Grove, "that there is something fundamentally different afoot. It's time to sit up and take notice."

Paying Attention

Once, we attended an event where Grove was speaking. When he was asked the secret of his success, he leaned forward and said, in his prominent German accent, "I have very big ears!"

Throughout his career Grove was known for bypassing middle management to engage front line employees in conversation... and most of the conversation involved him listening to their needs, concerns, opinions, and suggestions. The reason? Front line employees are the ones closest to the customer. This is not just a discipline for the CEO—middle managers as well need to be engaged in listening hard to both front line employees and customers, because that is usually where the future first reveals itself. And it is this discipline of listening that gives you confidence in seeing what lays ahead.

If you are a leader who is driving change from the Strategic Option, you have to pay attention to a number of things:

1. The customers, who insure your company's survival.

2. The regulatory environment, where laws can alter the competitive landscape in a single legislative session.

3. Complementary businesses, upon whom your organization relies for products, goods, and services.

4. Competitors, who may anticipate the future first themselves or may be making strategic mistakes your company must avoid.

Each of these entities, including competitors, are actually resources which must be leveraged for a vision to be realized.

As we interviewed Tom Cousins' colleagues, we heard time and again about how crucial his championing and articulating of the vision for East Lake was in the transformation process. When others would feel discouraged or get caught up in minutiae, Cousins' great gift was to keep the vision out front, repeatedly. He was able to do this only because he listened—engaging residents, government officials, and his colleagues in serious, reflective conversation. Like Andy Grove, he had the biggest ears in the room.

Taking the Heat

If you are serious about driving change, you are going to encounter opposition. But once you have seen the future, your ability to stick to the vision can make or break your organization's ability to adapt and thrive.

Today, Steve Reinemund is the dean of the prestigious business schools at Wake Forest University. But his reputation was forged in the ranks of management of PepsiCo Corporation where he rose to the level of CEO. Perhaps his greatest achievement was during the mid to late 1980s when he oversaw the operations of Pizza Hut.

It's hard to believe now, but at one time Pizza Hut was not in the home delivery business. All of their chips were in the retail restaurant business, where they dominated the domestic pizza market. Domino's dominated the home delivery market, and they appeared beyond challenge.

Strategic Questions

Sit down with some of your colleagues and discuss these.

- What do we say yes to, that we should say no to?
- What does our customer really value?
- How are our competitors doing things differently than they used to?
- What new competitors have emerged?
- Who is our target audience, really?
- What workarounds have our frontline employees adopted that could teach us something?
- If we could create a list where we could be #1, what list would that be?
- What legacy will future leaders say we left behind for them?

But Reinemund saw potential for Pizza Hut to compete with Domino's. Furthermore, he saw the future—that growth and market share in the pizza business involved delivering pies to customers to enjoy in the privacy of their homes. He introduced the idea of home delivery to his team and was met with immediate opposition.

When we talked to Steve, he recounted how there was serious and sustained opposition to the idea within the ranks of Pizza Hut management. Why mess with a good thing, they reasoned? Worse, the franchisees wanted no part of it? Why change what they were doing—and doing well—and enter into competition with a fierce competitor like Domino's, putting their investments on the line?

But Reinemund pressed ahead, and nearly sank Pizza Hut—for a while during the transformation the company was losing a million dollars a month. But Reinemund was not deterred. He had seen the future. "Most people move along incrementally in their careers, and change comes slowly. But I knew we had the opportunity at this point for a truly transformational event, to truly transform a company. I believed this was not only our best but only choice. And when you are in a transformational experience it changes the whole way you think of what is achievable and possible."

The end result? After a rocky start, Reinemund's idea paid off in a big way. Profits grew from fifty-four million to one hundred seventy-five million. And, within two years, Pizza Hut had overtaken Domino's market share.

As a leader who sees the future, you must anticipate resistance from within. But you must refuse to wilt in the face of the friendly fire.

Distinguishing the Want-Tos From the Need-Tos

Andy Grove learned that during change there are two distinct periods in the early going. The first is chaos, when everything is changing and everything is up for grabs. This is the time to move quickly, because time is your friend. This is the time to experiment.

But then there is the Valley of Death, when the true cost of the change becomes clear and denial is no longer an option. It is a sort of grieving process, letting go of the past to embrace the future. It is a good thing. But it is immeasurably hard.

The temptation during the Valley of Death is to hold on to the "want-tos," the things you have done in the past, that have worked in the past and that you are really good at doing. They are a symbol of stability, a reminder of a much more comfortable past. But there is no reason to continue doing them, because the past does not exist anymore.

What you must do instead is to embrace the need-tos, those things that must be accomplished for change to occur and for the preferred future to be realized. There is nothing easy about this. But the only way vision takes hold is if you look at the daily activities of your team and ruthlessly assess if the focus is on the hard, strategic need-tos.

Clayton Christensen, a leading expert on innovation, describes the "innovator's dilemma" for companies that have been successful in the past. They know the pathway to that success but they don't know the pathway to the future. In fact, they are unable to separate the past and their successful formulas from what needs to change to insure future viability. Within the organization, there is little if any tolerance for failure and high pressure to follow the previously successful path. In other words, there is literally no context for innovation, no path forward. According to Christensen, the only way the innovator's dilemma can be resolved is if there is a willingness to break with the past and the courage to create intentional contexts where experimentation is encouraged and failure is tolerated.

This requires discipline—for you and your team. And it requires the willingness to confront—both your personal (and usually unconscious) denial of the need for change, and of those on your team who cling to want-tos.

Creating Unlikely Alliances

Embracing a vision of the future requires something else—being willing to embrace unlikely alliances, some of which may even involve competitors.

One of our Senior Partners at TAG Consulting is Rex Miller, acclaimed futurist and author. In the 1990s Rex was an executive in the commercial construction and real estate industry in Dallas. Once a week he was part of a breakfast roundtable of key players in the industry who discussed the challenges and obstacles each faced. The group soon realized that, even though they were from different segments of the industry and in some cases were competitors, they all were staring down the same problems. Gradually, they came to the conclusion that they were key players in a broken industry.

It shouldn't have been that way. Fresh technologies—including three dimensional modeling for construction projects—as well as a new emphasis on "Lean construction" (cutting time and cost from building processes) and sustainability were opening up possibilities for entirely new ways of doing business. The construction industry should have been in an exciting time of innovation and change. Instead, it was stuck stumbling its way towards the future doing business in old ways that had never worked that well to begin with.

The group began talking to others and eventually group members convened a high level meeting of executives to talk about their mutual frustrations and possible ways forward. These executives, normally competitors, found common ground as they diagnosed the root of the problem—an industry filled with distrust based on conflict and fragmentation. They also found common ground on another conclusion: reform efforts alone were not enough. The commercial construction and real estate world would have to be fundamentally transformed. The challenge was no less than to build a culture of trust.

The group—now calling itself Mindshift—continued to communicate and to attend conferences together. Gradually, walls began to tumble down. And when that happened, industry leaders began to see how to incorporate the new technological advances in their work.

Rex says that participants began to see the "potential of trust-based teams powered with Virtual Design and construction tools, reducing waste and improving performance through Lean practices, and commonly aligned by relationally structured contracts." Over time, the industry was truly transformed, replacing a culture of conflict and mistrust with collaboration and trust and embracing technological innovation.

Sutter Health is one of the nation's leading not-for-profit networks of community-based health care providers. In 2003, they were ready to mount an ambitious eight billion dollar expansion project. But the state of the construction industry at the time meant that the costs would approach two million dollars per hospital bed!

Dave Pixley, Sutter's CEO, knew something had to change. So he brought his key executives in and defined the reality. At $1,000 per square foot construction costs, their very business model was in danger.

Working together, Pixley and his team developed some truly game-changing new strategies, which include radical new innovations in the areas of:

1. Team selection: Instead of putting together a motley crew of potential competitors, all of the parties involved would be selected on the basis of their fit with the team and their commitment to the project as a whole.

2. Contracts: Instead of an assortment of incentivized contracts which could turn should-be collaborators into competitors, there would be one single agreement.

3. Full disclosure: All contractors would be kept up to date on all aspects of the project, including the business plan itself!

4. Collaborative design: There would be a common location and common technological platforms which would enable contractors to share ideas, best practices, and timely questions.

It was a risky strategy, and required buy-in from a lot of skeptical parties. But it worked. The first project under the new approach was the Camino Medical Project in California. Stunningly, the project came in *six months early and nine million dollars under budget*!

In the Strategic Option, you must bring about a preferred future as a team-builder, but not just in the conventional sense. Teams that accomplish a strategic vision are often made up of unlikely bedfellows—partners, collaborators, folks who normally don't sit at the same table, and sometimes even competitors. You should always look to make connections, create alliances, and think creatively about who should be on the team and at the table. As Rex Miller says, there are always "dots waiting to be connected," and you need to be intentional about connecting those dots.

As important as anticipating the future and leveraging resources is for the Strategic Option, you can still fail to bring about a compelling vision unless you communicate with passion and clarity. Next, we'll take a look at what it takes to be that kind of communicator.

Chapter Five
Communicate Your Mission With Clarity

In the first two chapters about the Strategic Option we have focused on the importance of strategy and vision. To recap, vision answers the question "Where Are We Going?" while strategy addresses the question "What do we need to do to stay relevant?" Important stuff, to be sure.

But the fact is that the most compelling vision and the best strategy do not guarantee that your leadership will be successful. The missing, vital ingredient answers the question "Why are we doing what we're doing?" This is clarity of mission—communicating over and over again who you are and what you're all about. As a leader using the Strategic Option, you cannot over communicate, as long as that communication is crystal clear. While your organization and department need clarity, the clarity of mission starts with you.

Clarity drives behavior and performance. When the people you lead and serve are the beneficiaries of your clear communication about what's most important they will know how to act and respond when faced with a choice, a dilemma, or an ethical decision. Over time and given repeated clear communication the right behavior becomes second nature.

Think of the Disney employee who left his security guard post to snap a photo of two elderly ladies. Think of the Nordstrom employee who delivered a tailored and dry cleaned suit to the hotel room of a customer who had a crucial business meeting the next morning and had forgotten to pack correctly. And think of the Zappos.com employees who tracked down the names and phone numbers of late night pizza delivery places in the hometowns of customers who dialed up their call center. And keep in mind that Zappos is an online shoe store.

In each case the employees were crystal clear about their mission. In Disney's case, it is to provide a captivating experience to every guest—to make people happy. For Nordstrom, it is providing over the top customer service. For Zappos.com it is having EVERY customer say "That was the best customer service experience I have ever had." Their employees act instinctively to fulfill the mission. But this only happens because the mission and vision of each organization is ingrained in the hearts and minds of all of their associates.

So, what does it take to communicate with clarity?

Talk About The Future You Are Shaping Together

We had the opportunity to spend a day with Truett Cathey, the founder of the immensely popular Chick-fil-A restaurant chain. Founded as the Dwarf Grill in 1946, the restaurant pioneered the concept of the mall food court in 1967 as Chick-fil-A (it's hard to believe, but before then mall owners thought no one would shop where they would have to smell fast food). Due to his strong Christian faith, Cathey mandates that none of his stores are open on Sunday. In spite of this fact, the chain usually leads all other food court competitors in each mall. In 2010, Cathey celebrated forty-two consecutive years of rising profits for Chick-fil-A and nearly 1,500 stores across the nation. All of this success is built on a simple sandwich.

The legendary Chick-fil-A sandwich is incredibly tasty—at least we think so. It is also incredibly simple—a boneless chicken breast lightly fried in a signature blend of spices, nestled between halves of a hot buttered bun and adorned with a single "perfectly positioned" pickle. Simple, clean, clear. We found Truett Cathey himself to be equally clear about his mission, beliefs, and passions. Surprisingly, they have little to do with a wonderful chicken sandwich (or his equally wonderful waffle fries).

Truett Cathey's passion is for children, the next generation. His own three children have followed him into the family business, but Cathey's impact has extended to hundreds and even thousands of children outside of his biological family. His WinShape Foundation "helps shape winners" by supporting youth through scholarships and other programs. In partnership with Berry College, WinShape provides between twenty and thirty scholarships a year with amounts up to $32,000. Chick-fil-A provides scholarships to all young employees who log two years of service with the company.

WinShape Homes comprises eight foster care homes each of which care for up to twelve children with two foster parents. The goal is to provide care for these kids with a positive family environment. WinShape camps are two-week residential summer adventures which are oriented around character building and relationship creating activities. And WinShape Retreat on the campus of Berry College hosts marriage enrichment retreats, church and corporate conferences, and the WinShape girls' camps.

But Cathey's philanthropy is not just about a checkbook or a foundation. He told us that his greatest joy is the dozens of foster grandchildren he has gotten to know and in whose lives he has invested. In fact, we met with him the day after he received the

Martin Luther King, Jr. Award. On a regular basis Cathey and his family brought kids from the WinShape Homes into their own home for a few nights to share conversation, popcorn, hot chocolate and cookies. Cathey is in touch with many if not most of these kids, even as they grow into adulthood.

Read one of his several books, look at the Chick-Fil-a website or, even better, www.truettcathey.com or, best of all, visit with the man like we did and one message is crystal clear—what matters most is not profit, market share, or chicken, but rather faith, family, and investing in the next generation. Truett Cathey has built a great business on not just a delectable sandwich but a simple and clear mission communicated over and over via print, training, Internet, personal investment, and financial resources. The WinShape Foundation sums it up: "to help shape winners."

While your focus may not be on either chicken or children, you must make sure that the values and mission that drive your organization are so clear that your colleagues and employees feel that they are being called to do nothing less than change the world.

Talk About Who Your Customer Is

Zappos.com is one of the great success stories of Internet retailing. An online shoe and clothing store, Zappos began in 1999 and in 2009 grossed over one billion dollars in sales. Later that year, Zappos was acquired by Amazon.com in an all stock deal valued at more than 1.2 billion dollars. Over 60 percent of its customers are repeat buyers. Zappos specializes in niche shoe markets, including hard to find, oddly sized and vegan shoes. But, it's not about the shoes.

Zappos has what can only be described as a fanatical culture of customer service. Like many companies, Zappos' stated goal is to provide the best customer service in their industry. But they do more than talk about it. Zappos offers free shipping both ways, an unheard of 365 day return policy, and a call center that is open 24/7. All new hires in the corporate office are required to participate in a four-week customer service course which includes two weeks working the phones in the call center.

The new employees are given full salary during this orientation. At the end of the four weeks, startlingly, each employee is offered $3,000 to leave the company immediately. The goal is to insure that those who stay aren't there for the money but rather the cause. Ninety-nine percent of the new employees turn the offer down.

Every year, Zappos publishes a "Culture Book" which is made up of contributions from employees describing how much the company's culture and values means to them. All of this is driven by the stated core value of "delivering WOW through service." And it is captured in the crystal clear objective that each customer will leave every interaction with Zappos saying, "That was the best customer service experience I ever had."

Is it working? Zappos claims that its success is built on word of mouth and referrals (hence the extremely high 60 percent return customer metric). Experts on viral Internet marketing constantly cite Zappos as a prime example.

And, consider the stories! Take a minute to Google "Zappos customer service" or study blogs written by and for relationship marketing professionals and you uncover the mother lode of over the top customer service anecdotes. Like the call center employees we mentioned who found pizza delivery places for callers half a continent away. And like the guest who checked into the Mandalay Bay Hotel in Las Vegas and realized she had forgotten her shoes.

So she called Zappos (located in nearby Henderson, NV), from whom she had purchased the forgotten pair. Unfortunately, they were out of stock in her size. What happened next is extraordinary. Zappos employees went out to a nearby mall, found the shoes in the customer's color and size, purchased them, and delivered them to her hotel. All for free.

Tony Hsieh is the founder and CEO of Zappos and the author of the company's story *Delivering Happiness*. As he tells the story, a few years into Zappos' run he and the company's other leaders decided to reevaluate their corporate goals. "Did we just want to be about profit, or about something bigger?" The outcome of the discussions was that customer service would be the number one priority for real.

And this led to clarity as to the identity of the company's target market: its existing customers. Hsieh and his team knew that if they provided outrageous service to its customers, then "our customers would do our marketing for us." A 1.2 billion acquisition suggests that the strategy was a good one.

What's striking as you study Zappos is how relentlessly they communicate their mission. The "Culture Book." Blogs by company leaders and rank and file employees. Their website. New employee orientation. Hsieh's book. It is impossible to be around anything to do with Zappos and not get that their overwhelming priority is providing incredible experiences for their customers.

Similarly, the team leading the East Lake Villages transformation never stopped talking about their "customers"—the residents, particularly the children, of East Lake. And the children who would follow. Tom Cousins and team kept the mission front and center for years, never wavering from the central message: transform every aspect of East Lake.

When you operate in the Strategic Option, you must address this question: Who is your customer and what will it take to get them, please them, keep them, and get them to help us market our product, good, or service?" And then communicate this with relentless clarity, using every means at their disposal. Your customer may be your co-worker. Your customer may be a team or a department. Your customer may even be your boss!

Talk About Your "Core Score"

The writer Marcus Buckingham spent two decades studying great business leaders and came to the conclusion that they have one thing in common—they know how to keep things simple.

One of the things you can communicate with simplicity is what Buckingham calls the "core score," the most important metric of a particular organization, department, or team. Every organization must measure many things—profit margin, market share, employee retention—just to name a few. But great companies are clear about the most important metric—the "core score."

Buckingham cites the example of the Best Buy home electronics chain. Several years ago, Best Buy executives determined that their core strength was their "blue shirts," in-store employees, the most customer-facing ones. The core score, therefore, was Best Buy's number of employees engaged in the company's values. So, how to measure that?

Best Buy leaders went to work and developed a series of twelve simple questions designed to elicit degree of employee engagement. Employees can look at the questions as a mirror—how engaged am I? And supervisors can evaluate their employees in light of the questions—how engaged is she? The key is that everyone, from CEO to frontline employee, knows that out of all the things that could be measured "engagement" is the most important one.

If you are using the Strategic Option, you know your core score. You know what your team or department has to achieve. You know what your organization is trying to achieve. And you talk about it all the time. Your employees and teammates know it as well. The core score is inescapable.

Talk About Your Key Products

The legendary thought leader Peter Drucker used to say that every business must answer two questions before it does anything else: What business are we in? And who is our customer?

Part of answering "What business are we in?" is knowing what are your key products, those goods or services that provide a differentiation point from your competition and a competitive edge in the marketplace.

Seth Godin has become known as a marketing and branding guru, skillfully leveraging his books and blog and breaking new ground when it comes to capitalizing on intellectual capital, making the business world better and turning a profit all at once. His blog is ranked by *AdAge* as the number one marketing blog, out of the 960 it tracks. And marketing professionals are notoriously easily bored.

He is a prolific writer and blogger and reader/performer of his own E-books. The man churns out product. But read his stuff—engaging, all of it—and one thing becomes clear. He is repeating the same thing over and over, in ever more creative ways.

Godin's original, great idea had to do with "permission marketing." His thinking ran like this: the end of the "TV-industrial complex" was ushered in by the rise of the Internet and cable television and the public's ability to get their information from a nearly endless array of options, not just broadcast TV, the local newspaper and the New York Times. As a result, consumers have more power. Marketers can no longer command attention; they must request it and compete for it. Spam doesn't work; lousy customer service will run you out of business, and you'd better keep your promises.

> **A Problem is Strategic When....**
> - It is driven by changes to the external environment (new competition, changing demographics, and so forth)
> - It requires an innovative way to address it
> - It is central to your organization's values or mission
> - It is a priority for the whole organization

In other words, marketers must ask for permission and once they have received it keep their promises. Godin makes this point and shows how to carry it out. And that is pretty much what he does.

To be sure, his metaphors change—"sneezers" and "purple cows" and the "IdeaVirus" and the like. But his key product is the concept of permission marketing and his ability to show his readers and listeners how to offer customers experiences and products that are "anticipated, personal, and relevant."

And that's what you do when you use the Strategic Option —you know your key product and find as many creative ways to talk about it as you can. You know what business you're in and you make sure everyone who works with and for you does as well.

Talk About Your Hedgehog Concept

The writer Jim Collins popularized the idea of the hedgehog concept. When we heard Collins speak at a gathering of CEOs several years ago, he explained the idea he had made famous in his books *Built to Last* and *Good To Great* and that was built on the differences between the wily, multi-tasking fox and the focused one-action-only hedgehog. Every day the fox and the hedgehog battled. The fox always tried something new. The hedgehog never deviated from his plan. Eventually, the hedgehog won.

Every organization, if it is going to be truly great and truly long lasting must find the point of intersection between three circles, which represent three questions:

1. What are we most passionate about?

2. What can we do better than anyone else?

3. What drives our economic engine?

Once you have answered all three questions and found the places where they intersect, you have found your hedgehog concept. The hedgehog concept tells you what you should say yes to and, just as if not more important, what you should say no to. Your hedgehog concept tells you where you should spend resources, time, blood, sweat, and tears and what you should let pass. Your hedgehog concept tells you where your organization can become great, if you remain focused.

If you are reading this book and your organization has not found its hedgehog concept, prioritize doing that. Whether you have influence over an entire enterprise or just a department or division, look at your span of power and find the intersection of your passion, your core competencies, and your ability to make a profit.

Once you have done that, evaluate your operations, budgeting, goals and priorities and feed those things that fit with the hedgehog concept. Starve those things that don't. And talk at length, with frequency, and with great clarity about why you have done those things.

Don't Just Talk, Act!

For all of your talking, you know that your actions speak louder than your words. Always look for crucial moments when you can take a deliberate action that will communicate volumes.

Marcus Buckingham distinguishes between "symbolic actions" and "systemic actions." Systemic actions are deeply consequential deeds that cause those who witness them to question their fundamental beliefs and values and to change their action. We will have much to say about systemic actions in the section of this book where we discuss the Transformational Option.

Symbolic actions are important as well. These are deeds that show your colleagues and employees what the future can look like. They arrest people's attention and reorient their thinking.

Buckingham uses the example of former New York City mayor Rudolph Giuliani, who inherited leadership of a city gripped by a crime wave and a crumbling infrastructure. One of his first actions was to enforce a strict ban on "squeegee men," homeless guys who assaulted cars stalled in traffic with dirty squeegees streaming filthy water and demanded money to "clean" the trapped motorists' windows. The action really didn't change New York all that much, but its purpose was symbolic. By eliminating a nuisance that all New Yorkers with a car despised Giuliani pointed the way to the better future that he had promised.

Similarly, Giuliani convened twice a week meetings of one hundred senior police officers where he confronted them with the city's most recent crime data and demanded that they defend their responses to it. The stated purpose of the meeting was to elicit accountability and transparency. But the real symbolic effect was that the routines of these busy and powerful leaders were disturbed and their futures called into question.

Strategic, decisive actions at well-chosen moments point the way to the future, show the possibility of a different way of living, and, most of all, clearly communicate the chosen path of an organization. They demand attention through their clarity and focus.

We've talked about strategy, vision and clarity of mission. Carry these out and you are headed for success as a Strategic Option leader. But these alone are insufficient. You will need to build, lead, and empower the right people. How do you do that? Glad you asked!

Section Three
The Tactical Option

Chapter Six
Selecting People

Several years ago, TAG Consulting had the opportunity to host Jim Collins, whose hedgehog concept we discussed in the last chapter, at a gathering of our staff, clients and prospective strategic partners.

Our anticipation was high as we gathered at a beautiful resort in the Rocky Mountains on a gorgeous winter day. We sat around tables set up in a horseshoe fashion and spent the day hearing from and dialoguing with this great leadership thinker. It was a day to remember. Collins said a lot of things we are still thinking about and applying. But one statement stood out above all the others.

When it comes to selecting people for your team, Collins said, "Never hire anyone you will have to manage."

Wow. At once provocative and seemingly impossible to implement, the meaning of what Collins said comes clear only after some thought. Of course, organizations must be managed— whether they are in the for-profit or not-for-profit sector. We have to develop and employ systems and processes. But when it comes to the people, the very best team members are those who are going to naturally do what their role requires with a minimum of interference or direction. Microsoft has long had a hiring mantra that simply says "hire smart people who can think."

So, how do we select the right people for the team? This most important Tactical Option skill is our subject in this chapter.

The Most Basic Question

Good answers begin with the right questions. So we will start with a basic question, one that may have you scratching your head: **Why do I bring people on teams?** Why do I hire employees, choose board members, or fill out committee rosters?

The answer seems obvious, right? You bring people on teams to get tasks done, to generate income for the enterprise, maybe even to provide a valuable social service. But, let's dig deeper. Beyond the obvious answers, why do you interview people for positions, select them, perhaps compensate them, and then provide leadership and direction and opportunity for them? We believe there are three answers.

You Bring People on Teams to Fulfill The Promise of a Role With Excellence

When the typical busy manager interviews potential employees, she is asking these questions: "Can this person do the job? And if so, how well will they do the job?" If the answers feel right and if there is evidence that this is the case we say, "Let's hire this guy. Because he can probably do the job. And because he can probably do the job well."

But the dirty little secret is that you often settle for less than excellence in the selection process. And this is simply because you are neither asking the right questions nor listening for the right answers.

Here's the most important question: *"Is this person we are interviewing uniquely and naturally designed to do what we are hiring them to do?"*

In other words, if we were not paying this person would they as a matter of course be demonstrating the kinds of behavior that would make performance in this position remarkable? The question is the same if we are considering them for a volunteer position. This is a much deeper question than: Do they have the right degree? Have they punched the right ticket? Do they have the requisite experience generally expected of someone interviewing for a position like this?

A good receptionist smiles all the time, even in her off hours, right? A successful therapist is a person marked by empathy. A high-grossing salesperson loves to be around people even in her off hours.

We were sitting around the table with a leadership team of a successful company. We were chatting with Misse, an executive assistant who was known for her high level organizational skills. "Misse," we asked her, "can you pinpoint a time in your life when you were first recognized as being an organized person?"

Her answer was immediate. "When I was a toddler, I would creep to the family's food cupboard, take out all of the canned goods, and then place them back in the cupboard, organized by color."

As a toddler! You see, you are hard-wired to do something— maybe a few things—extraordinarily well. And if you examine your life, you will see that you have always been doing these things. So, as we hire people, we will match what we need in the position to a person who naturally does those things.

This is part of the power of Malcolm Gladwell's "10,000 hour rule." Gladwell argues that the truly exceptional have practiced their craft—be it playing the piano, striking a golf ball, piloting a plane, learning to lead—for roughly 10,000 hours over a period of ten years. True greatness begins after 10,000 hours. We would add no one does something over a decade for 10,000 hours unless, at some deep level, they *want* to. In hiring, look for people who are already doing naturally what you need them to do for and with you.

Bring People on Teams to Fulfill The Promise of Your Mission

Every excellent organization—the kind that you want to build—has its daily activities rooted in a sense of mission. Mission is the unique reason that your organization exists—the specific "calling" you have as a team. You bring people on teams so that this mission can be accomplished, since you can't do it all on your own.

In the same way that you select people based on their natural fit for the requirements of the specific position, you should select people who naturally fit the overall mission of the organization.

If you are running a not-for-profit that feeds homeless people, you will look for someone who cares about the issues of addiction, broken families, and economic inequality and has demonstrated those concerns in concrete ways. If you are running a lobbying firm which specializes in pacifist causes, you are not looking for a gun collector!

Two clues are important in determining natural mission fit. First, is biography. What does this person's life story tell us about her concerns and passions? Second, is performance. Does this person demonstrate allegiance to values that are related to our mission, or is it all just talk?

When we interviewed Chuck Knapp from the East Lake team, he spoke passionately about mission fit when describing what type of person fit in well during the community's transition. "First, the person has to have a heart for this. Second, they have to be a roll up your sleeves and get dirty type of person. Third, they have to work and play well with others."

Each of these characteristics—a demonstrated track record of commitment, humility, willingness to be a team player, and strong work ethic—are at the core of the East Lake Foundation's mission.

Carol Naughton was every bit as passionate as Chuck Knapp. A fan of Jim Collins, like we are, she borrowed his idea of getting the right people in the right seat on the bus. "We had to have the right people for the team—and not just the right people in the abstract. They had to be right for their roles and they had to have the right values. The goal—which we never allowed ourselves to imagine would not be accomplished—was more important than any one person."

Scott Pioli is the general manager of the Kansas City Chiefs in the National Football League. He took on the challenge of revitalizing one of the NFL's most moribund franchises after years of championship success making player personnel decisions for the New England Patriots. One of Pioli's best friends is Thomas Dimitroff, general manager for the Atlanta Falcons. When both were very junior employees for NFL teams (Dimitroff was a member of the *grounds crew* for the Cleveland Browns) they struck up a friendship and began to talk about their philosophies of selecting people.

Dimitroff told *Sports Illustrated*, "I think Scott and I both believe it's much easier to build a team when you are throwing character issues out the window. There are some very talented players coming into this league... and the easy thing to do is to bring in the most talented players whether they fit or don't fit. You can win that way, no question about it." "But," said Pioli, continuing his friend's thought, "the key is sustainability. Do you want to build a team that will win once and then implode? The job is to make the difficult decisions so you can build the kind of team that can be in position to win every single year."

Selecting people based on mission fit is the best way to insure long-term success.

We Bring People on Teams To Fulfill The Promise of Providing Solutions

Every person is uniquely designed to provide solutions for certain kinds of problems. This truth is central to leading with the Tactical Option, which of all the sides of the Leadership Triangle most deals with problems.

Think about it. We bet that there is a certain kind of problem— perhaps one that bedevils and frustrates other people—which you excel at solving. What appears to be a Gordian knot to others is something you can untangle effortlessly.

This is true for everybody. Misse is designed to organize and run logistics. We bet that when her company is preparing for its next offsite her brain is already whirring about location, catering, transportation arrangements, entertainment, seating charts, and lodging.

What's more, you *enjoy* solving the problems you are meant to solve. Where others would tear their hair out, you are energized. As a matter of fact, you actively seek opportunities to solve the problems you are gifted at solving because the end result gives you a feeling of accomplishment, well-being, and pride.

Your organization has problems (so does ours!). And out there are potential team members who would love nothing more than to work with you to solve those problems. They are already offering such solutions in other areas of their lives for free!

How do you identify the people who are uniquely designed to provide the solutions to the challenges your organization is facing? You identify people who are providing the same kinds of solutions in other places.

So, the job interview is not so much focused on academic degree or lines on a résumé as it is on a conversation. "What kind of challenges have been most invigorating for you? Tell me about a time when you provided a specific solution for that kind of challenge. What was that experience like? Did you seek out the challenge? How did you feel afterwards?"

You're looking for passionate, engaged responses, not "Oh, my boss assigned it to me and when I had figured it out I felt pretty good, I guess." You want to hear "Yep, I had wanted to slay that giant for a long time and when I got the chance it was a blast and I was on a success high for a week afterwards!"

We want to offer two practical tools for getting the right people in the right jobs. First, is Intentional Difference™, a concept that we at TAG have found indispensable. Second, is a list of qualities that describe the very best selectors of people.

Intentional Difference™

Through our executive coaching practice we have interviewed, advised, and studied hundreds of success-proven leaders. As a result, our database contains research on a variety of leaders across a wide range of industries. Recently, we focused our attention on unpacking that data to discover what common traits emerged as distinct and quantifiable in successful leaders.

The data revealed that the leaders in our database were all very different. They had various combinations of talent themes as revealed by the strengths assessment tool we used. There was a mixture of introverts and extroverts and feeling and thinking leaders. Leaders had a variety of leadership styles. All of the leaders had numerous areas of development opportunities according to their performance feedback reports. Some leaders had stellar feedback and others had not so stellar feedback from peer, supervisor, and subordinates. There was a staggering proliferation of differences. The only thing we could say with some degree of certainty was that the most successful leaders seemed to have virtually nothing in common!

So, we looked again, but instead of looking at them as successful leaders who had a distinct and different quality, we looked at them as individuals who may have somehow tapped into a common quality that transformed them into successful leaders.

Then, we made a remarkable discovery that we are excited to share with you. They all had exactly one thing in common—they had discovered the power of their Intentional Difference™!

Here's what we mean. When it comes to your performance as a leader, 85 percent of what you do, most people are capable of doing (don't be insulted!). Ten percent of what you are capable of doing select people can do or be trained to do. But 5 percent of what you are capable of doing only you—you alone—can do.

This 5 percent is your Intentional Difference™ (I.D. for short). Willful, determined, and disciplined use of your I. D. will radically transform your life and leadership.

This 5 percent (your I.D.) of what you are capable of consists of six components: Talent, Skills and Knowledge, Knowledge, Experience, Passions, and Outcomes.

Talent is the unconscious, observable, and reliable patterns of how you think, feel, or behave. Talent is our innate hard wiring. In computer lingo, it is our human "operating system." It translates data into ideas, emotions, and action.

Skills are rehearsed behaviors that, when combined with recurring patterns, produce outstanding results. Popular belief says skills are acquired. We disagree. We believe skills emerge. In the context of our talent, the skills that improve and get much better over time are those that are natural expressions of our talent. The five- year-old that sings in perfect pitch. The child with no arms that plays the Cello with his feet. The four-year-old that instinctively knows how to use a golf club. These are real examples of talent finding its natural expression in a demonstrated skill.

Knowledge is increased awareness of how, when, and where your natural patterns should be applied. We learn by doing, and not doing. When talent is present learning is ubiquitous. There are cues and clues everywhere!

Experience is wise historical perspective on what decisions and actions bring what results. Talent multiplies time. A non-talented person doing the same task as a talented person will take longer.

Yes, some of the efficiency is due to ability. More so, however, it is due to how talent makes experience more cumulative. The more the talented five-year-old sings, the more precise she becomes at adding the thrill to her voice at just the right moment.

Passions are what energize us. They are rooted in our core values. They are the things that drive us and that make us feel fully alive. Many people pursue passions outside of work. Those who are able to make money by following their passions have truly discovered their vocation (or calling)!

Outcomes are consistent repeated performance in a task or activity at above average standard. We never come to know or celebrate an average performer as we would the above average performer. When we speak of a person being talented, they are consistently performing above the standard of most others. Talent ignites a desire and ability to outperform others.

In summary, talent initiates and multiplies our skills, knowledge, experience, passions, and outcomes. Lance Armstrong had to learn to ride a bicycle just like the rest of us. However, for him because of his innate talent, the thrill of learning to ride stirred up and fueled performance traits (skills, knowledge, experience, passions, and outcomes) for him in a very different way than for most of us.

Let's put it all together in this equation:

Talent (Skills + Knowledge + Experience + Passions + Outcomes) = Your Intentional Difference™!

Before you go much further in this book, stop and ask yourself—what are the things that I naturally do and get better at doing in an observable and measurably unique way...what is my Intentional Difference™?

Knowing your Intentional Difference™ means you have identified, owned, and understood how your prevailing talent plus your unique traits of skills, knowledge, experience, passions, and outcomes help or hinder you.

To be successful, you must access your I.D. That means learning how to unleash the full power of your talent plus your skills, knowledge, experience, passions and outcomes. More on how to do this later when we introduce you to the Intentional Difference Process™. For now, just know that there are immeasurable benefits that come from understanding your I.D.

We think of three clients when we think of the benefits of understanding Intentional Difference™.

The first client was an organization led by a "dream team" of executives. These were some of the most high capacity leaders we have been around, truly leaders in their industry. They were great strategists, communicators, and visionaries.

Yet our work with their organization revealed that down-line employees felt disconnected from not only their leaders but also the larger purpose of the organization. The leaders were shocked when we told them that their employees weren't sure where the organization was headed and that they felt that their managers did not communicate effectively. After all, the leaders thought, we know our talents—we have done the test. We know our personality type, we know how to engage the introvert. We even have the results from our employee engagement survey, and they are not bad at all!

Ah, but focusing on the I.D., revealed something telling. The team's prevailing patterns were unbalanced. They had tons of ideas, plenty of visionaries, daily practice, lots of experience, and a surplus of effective communicators. But they had no one—and we mean no one—on the team with talents and traits that drive execution and implementation. Not an administrator or logistics expert (they needed a Misse!) in the bunch!

The result was that the management team was always ten steps ahead of everybody else in the organization in terms of vision and communication. And so their down-line employees

Tactical Questions

Sit down with some of your colleagues and discuss the following questions.

- What are our core traits (have you discovered the Intentional Difference™ of each team member yet)?

- What percentage of my time do I spend intentionally using my prevailing talents/traits?

- What can I do differently in order to spend most of my time using my core talents/traits?

- How can we improve our productivity as a team?

- What additional skills or talents/traits do we need to bring on to our team?

- What incentives or rewards would better leverage our traits? Motivate my team members?

felt bewildered, left behind, and disrespected. The solution? Add people whose I.D. included prevailing talents and traits that share task ownership and drive operational execution for the team! They did so and are enjoying success today.

Our second client had just completed a successful transition to the leadership of a new CEO—a best-case example of succession planning. The new leader, in his early months on the job, inherited a healthy organization and a high-performing team. Frankly, we loved working with this organization! Employee satisfaction scores were high. The focus groups we conducted were positive. The bottom line was healthy. The process of working with them was fun, engaging, and rewarding. Today we follow up with them monthly, and they are growing and going from strength to strength.

Their data explained why. They have a synergistic team profile. Their I.D. includes prevailing talents and traits which make sure the work gets done. Creating new ways of doing things was natural for them—it didn't feel like we were imposing something on them. This team is motivated by a sense of ethical grounding. They possess motivational skills (often related to sales) which gets people on board. This was reinforced by knowledge of how to value and reinforce significant relationships and relational intimacy.

Taken together, this team's individual team member I.D. profile were in perfect balance. This was a healthy leadership team, leading a high-performing organization due to the fact that they had executives whose prevailing patterns were in synergy.

The third client we are thinking of was an entirely different matter. Where client number two was an example of reinforcing talents and traits, this client was a case study of talents and traits on a high-speed collision course. We sensed the tension when we first sat down with the eleven key leaders on the team.

The tension was reflected in the organization's subpar performance, its widespread employee dissatisfaction, and the obvious morale issues we witnessed just walking through the building.

The tension and unhealthiness found a face in the CEO. We had been told in the focus groups we conducted that he was heavy-handed and authoritarian. The organization was considering a major capital project and his approach at the planning meeting had been to say "Here's what I want and how I want it done. Let's get to work." And then he walked out of the room.

When it came time for our meeting, the CEO was late. He sat in his chair obviously disengaged, playing with his smart phone, and rarely making eye contact with anyone. His team was a mess. And, once again their I.D.s revealed why.

This team of eleven had five members who had the same one prevailing talent—two times the national average. They were great strategists. It's hard to get multiple Strategists to agree on a common goal. Five out of eleven were people who needed to get a lot done, they were achievement-oriented people—the same problem. Five out of eleven had very strong relational traits, but each one had different rules for relationships. It got worse.

Four out of eleven were self-assured (SIX times the national average), meaning each thinks he or she is the measure of what is right. Three of the eleven were exacting and uncompromising.

No one on the team had prevailing talents and traits that made them positive or uplifting. No one had prevailing talents and traits that made any of them peace makers. No one on the team had prevailing talents and traits that caused them to even want to think about working on creating greater intimacy on the team.

One person on the team had a great capacity for empathy. We assumed that person was on the maximum allowable dose of Prozac!

It wasn't that these were bad people. But they were a bad team because they had unbalanced talents and traits and the talents and traits they did have were destined to be on a collision course. Working with them was demoralizing, an uphill slog, like pulling teeth. And they weren't willing to take up the challenge of learning how to optimize the very different talent mix on the team. We won't work with them again.

When you are engaged in the Tactical Option work of putting together teams, make sure they are balanced, diverse, and stable, loaded with talents and traits which reinforce each other. We highly recommend you consider learning how to use Intentional Difference™ as a process to assess your current team and decide if there are any talents and traits you need to add or reinforce.

What Makes A Great People-Picker?

Before we move on from this topic of positioning people as part of the Tactical Option toolbox, we want to encourage you with a list of qualities to aspire for and develop in your own leadership. These are the talents and traits that make for a great selector of teams!

Great People-Pickers are Success-Intuitive

If you are a great selector of people you can look at a potential team member and see what makes them tick. You see their passion, understand how their past has shaped them, have a sense of their dreams, and can visualize their future success.

Great People-Pickers are Placement-Aware

The best selectors of people see exactly where and on which team a person can fit. You will look at a potential team member and know the right seat on the bus for that person, the perfect role that will tee them and the team up for success.

When Paul Azinger took over as Captain of the United States Ryder Cup golf team prior to the 2008 competition, the fortunes of the Americans were at an all time low. In this biannual competition between twelve golfers representing Europe and twelve representing America, the Europeans had won nine straight times, often convincingly. This was in spite of the fact that in most of those competitions the Americans had the most talented individual golfers. When Azinger assumed leadership of the U.S. team he knew something had to change. He started with the selection process.

For years, the selection process for the U.S. team had been about finding the most talented golfers playing at the highest level at the time of selections and putting them on the team. The idea was that superior talent would win out. The strategy had failed nine consecutive times. So, Azinger changed things up drastically. His most important tactical decision was to choose the team based on team cohesion and chemistry instead of talent alone.

So, he chose the players he thought had the chance to form the strongest relationships. Startlingly, this included four first time Ryder Cup competitors; fully one-third of his team were newbies—this for an incredibly intense and competitive event where everyone assumed experience was crucial.

Then he borrowed a page from the Navy SEALS and grouped his players into three "pods" based on what he perceived to be emotional and temperamental compatibility.

Finally, Azinger did his best to establish competitive matchups and pairings that played to each player's strengths.

All of this was unconventional, even radical. The end result? The United States defeated the Europeans by a convincing five points.

Great People-Pickers are Future-Oriented

As a good leader, you will see the future of your organization as well as your own future. A great people-picker sees the future of each team member. You can visualize not only their success and the success of the organization, but also the success of each individual.

And you will find ways to communicate this, inspiring vision and hope and pulling the best out of each team member. "After all," the team member thinks, "if my leader believes in me this much, why shouldn't I?"

When people can see a preferred vision of the future for themselves that includes success they are motivated to perform at a high level in the present.

Great People-Pickers are Unselfishly Opportunistic

Don Clifton had a great question that we use all the time when considering someone who works for and with us: "How can I help this person discover just how good, just how successful he or she can become?"

That's a profound question, isn't it? You see its power, don't you?

If you are always working to provide opportunities for those on your team, or for those you are considering for your team, each team member knows that his or her back is covered and they are free to engage in their work with passion and confidence. If I know that someone else is plotting my success, then I am free to work with abandon and joy, free of the need to watch over my shoulder or play organizational politics.

It is a wise leader who knows that providing opportunities for individuals on his team to use their natural talents and traits results in his own success in the long run. Effective leaders abandon themselves to the prevailing talents and traits of others.

Great People-Pickers are Time Conscious

The leaders at East Lake knew that time was everything. A confluence of people and decisions had to come together at once. There were a lot of moving parts and contingencies. The door to success was only opened for brief periods. And so the team knew that they had to seize every moment for its full potential.

The great Tactical Option leader knows that time is only on our side if we cause it to be so. Having selected a great team with balanced talents and traits, we keep one eye on the clock and one eye on the end goal as we empower our teams.

Chapter Seven
Building People

So, you've selected your dream team. The right people are in the right seats on the bus, your team's talents and traits are reinforcing one another, morale is high, and folks are fired up. What now? What do you do to build this group you have so carefully and thoughtfully selected, so that your dream team can win championships in your work?

In the last chapter, we framed our conversation around a question: Why do we hire people or recruit team members? That question leads naturally to another that will frame our discussion about team building: **Why do people work?**

It is more than just the need to earn a living and possibly provide for a family, important as those basic financial motivations are. Once the basic needs of life are met, what are the reasons a person will choose a particular job and stay at that particular job? It's all about winning prizes, but prizes that go far beyond financial success.

People Work to Gain the Prize of Personal Achievement

Our culture is rooted in a strong work ethic. Embedded deeply into the American consciousness is a respect for hard work and achievement. Embedded deeply into the human spirit is the desire to experience the satisfaction of a productive vocation that engages the mind and the heart, and sometimes the body. We were created to work, to achieve, to accomplish. If we don't work, we waste away.

We respect people who work this way, and we respect ourselves when we work this way. And we crave both the respect of others, but more important the deep satisfaction of self-respect.

People Work To Gain The Prize of Financial Stability

Not everyone is motivated by money. But virtually everyone is motivated by the things that money can provide—freedom, leisure, a life lived without fear of deprivation and want, flexibility, the ability to provide well for those who are dependent on us, the ability to meet the needs of those less fortunate. Not everyone is motivated by money, but few would turn down the offer of a healthy check!

Whether or not your job provides a high income, you are more than likely motivated to do your job well in hopes of maximizing that income and enjoying the benefits of financial security. And you hope that over time you will experience more than security, because more money means more freedom and flexibility and leisure and ability to invest your money in good works.

People Work to Gain the Prize of Purposeful Living

It is this aspect of the motivation to work that is easy to miss. Even if you have self-respect, the respect of others, and a measure of financial security you won't be fulfilled. Those things are essential, but they are not enough. The final reason we work is so that our labor is a part of something bigger than just the nature of the labor itself. We long for our lives to be connected to a broader purpose and a higher goal.

Let's say you are looking for a job. An offer comes your way and what stands out about it in your mind is neither the pay nor the benefits nor the opportunity for advancement. What you love is the schedule. You can't contain your excitement because the job is structured in such a way that you will work for four days and then have three days off.

Three days off! Think of all you can do with three days off! You can spend extra time with your newborn child. You can train for a marathon. You can enroll in classes and study for an advanced degree. You can spend more time volunteering at the nearby homeless shelter.

Or you are considering joining the board of a not-for-profit organization. What you love about the opportunity is that you would get the chance to spend time with the Executive Director, a person you have long admired. She is well known for investing relationally in her board members and you can see some areas where such a relationship could really grow and stretch you.

You see, your job provides the means and the pathway to accomplish things—social good, personal achievement, relational enhancement—that is bigger than the job itself. The things we really want are bigger and better than anything we can do tangibly in a particular job.

So, those are the reasons we work. And we are assuming that as you have built your team all of these things are available to each team member—social and self-respect, financial provision, and the opportunity to accomplish something bigger than just the job itself. But there's one thing missing.

Most of us don't want to do our jobs alone. Sure, there are exceptions, but most of us long to experience the joy of accomplishment and success with others. We long to be part of a team. And one of the most important skills for a leader exercising the Tactical Option is knowing how to build teams that can both achieve success and provide satisfaction and engagement for their members.

Let's start with how NOT to build a team. The work of Patrick Lencioni has been very helpful to us in thinking through this, particularly his **Five Dysfunctions of a Team.**

Lencioni argues that there are five things that can hamper the effectiveness and fulfillment of a team.

First is the *absence of trust.* In a team, your ability to do your job is to some degree dependent on others on the team. You need to be able to trust that they will keep their word, share information with you, do their work and have the corporate interest at heart. Once this trust is broken we silo ourselves off, withhold information, and spend time and energy that could go into creative pursuits on worry and office politics.

Second is a *fear of conflict.* Maybe you don't like conflict as a function of your personality. Maybe you are afraid you will be exposed. Maybe the team leader gets freaked out by conflict and so spends all his time brokering compromises that leave everyone frustrated and no one happy. Whatever the reason, no one argues and so the team never advances.

Third is a *lack of commitment.* Nothing saps energy faster from a team than a member or two who are not carrying their weight or don't want to be there to begin with. Lack of commitment engenders mistrust, demotivation and resentment. And those things are poison to a team.

Another form of lack of commitment is failing to commit to the team itself. Lone Ranger team members who ignore suggestions, hoard information, and aren't willing to leave their silos to help a teammate can sow division and dissension on a team and kill performance.

The fourth dysfunction is *avoidance of accountability.* Accountability carries an unpleasant connotation—I worry that Big Brother or Sister is looking over my shoulder, inflicting slow death by a thousand nagging cuts. I worry that my performance will be judged wanting in comparison to others. I worry that my inadequacies will be exposed. I worry that my own agenda might be derailed and my own freedom curtailed.

And so I run from being evaluated or I fudge outcomes to put the best face on an unpleasant reality. And as a result no one is really sure whether or not they or the team are doing a good job.

The final dysfunction of a team is being *inattentive to results.* This is managerial cowardice, when people are rewarded for effort alone without due regard to outcomes. This saps healthy ambition and leaves everyone wondering "Now, exactly why did we spend all that time and effort doing that if no one cares and no one is rewarded for good work?"

That was a depressing survey, wasn't it? But we had to get it out of the way in order to get to the good, inspiring stuff— practical ways that, operating in the Tactical Option, you can build teams that accomplish great things, forge pleasing relationships, and leave team members energized and ready for more! It is as simple (and as challenging) as turning the Five Dysfunctions on their head.

And please note—these principles are not just for the marketplace. They apply to any scenario where it takes a team to accomplish a task—a sports team, a volunteer committee, a task force at a church.

Building Great Teams

Build The Team Around The Task

Perhaps you have read some of the writings of Douglas Smith and Jon Katzenbach on building teams. Their core insight is that building teams is not about team-building.

Huh?

What we mean is that what creates high-performing teams is not team-building exercises but rather creating a climate where three things happen:

- The team has a clear sense of mission and clearly defined goals.

- Everyone knows their role.

- Everyone is given freedom to use their talents and traits within the context of their role and the mission.

The best shot for this to happen for you is when you build your team not around the team itself, but around the task. This means that you will choose team members based on their experience at getting the kinds of results you are looking for. You will look for talents and traits that are congruent with your goals. And you will, at every turn, keep the task itself front and center.

Create a Climate of Trust

A climate of trust starts with the leader being trustworthy himself. Do you keep your promises, meet your commitments, honor your word, and provide the resources you have agreed to provide? Can you be relied on to perform yourself, to protect the team and its individuals, to never throw another team member under the bus to protect yourself? A trustworthy leader is the bedrock foundation of a trustworthy team.

In the East Lake story, trust was the irreducible minimum. Without a trustworthy team made up of trustworthy individuals, the transformation would never have happened. No one could have been more untrusting—at first—than Eva Davis. So the East Lake team responded in a trustworthy manner. Shirley Franklin and Greg Giornelli listened to her concerns and told her they appreciated her point of view. The team kept returning with the same tattered easel and pad presenting the same project, showing that no one was trying to pull a fast one. Tom Cousins—in his plainspoken way—kept saying the same things again and again and backed his words up with his actions.

Another aspect of trust is that the team knows that the leader is willing to serve as mentor as well as supervisor. A mentor is simply someone who invests in another person by providing knowledge, experience, and resources. The key element in a mentoring relationship is that the

A Problem is Tactical When...

- It is easily solved with the right expert (attorney, accountant, IT support, and so forth)

- It doesn't involve values, behaviors, or attitudes

- The solution won't cause any pain or loss

- It is focused on one department or team rather than the whole organization

- Trust is well-established

mentor says "I am for you as a person, as a professional—and I am willing to give you my time and resources and perspective to see you succeed." We'll do almost anything for that person. We trust them because we know they have our interests at heart.

One of the best examples of a mentor we have ever seen is Heather Wern, the director of food services in a busy cafeteria.

When Heather took the job she noticed that one of her employees performed with consistent excellence. So Heather began to give this woman more tasks and more responsibility. "With each new task I assigned her, she performed better than the task before," Heather told us.

One day, the woman stopped Heather in the cafeteria. "Miss Heather," said the worker, I just want to thank you for helping me." Heather's reply was immediate. "No," she said. "Thank *you* for helping me by being so good at your job!"

The woman's response was shocking. Instead of a smile, the woman broke into tears. Sobbing, body-shaking tears. Startled, Heather pulled the woman into her office in the back of the kitchen. And the employee's story unfolded, leaving Heather in tears as well.

"She told me that just prior to my coming to work in the cafeteria she had concluded that life was not worth living anymore. She made up her mind to end her life and was busy putting things in order and making plans for her suicide. But once I began giving her opportunities and calling on her to do more she began to reconsider. She began to wonder if there was some reason to live after all.

"I just want to thank you for saving my life, Miss Heather," she said again and again.

You see, this kind of mentoring creates trust, which is indispensable for your team. But where trust is lacking, look out!

We live in the suburbs of Washington, D.C. which means that we are treated daily to news and notes about the legendary local NFL franchise, the Washington Redskins. The Redskins are owned by a billionaire, Daniel Snyder, who makes no bones about his desire to have a Super Bowl-winning team and a dynasty franchise.

And Snyder puts his money where his mouth is. Aside from perhaps the Dallas Cowboys' Jerry Jones, no NFL owner has demonstrated a stronger commitment to paying lucrative salaries to free agent players with enticing reputations.

But the Redskins continually over-promise and under-deliver. Recently, the Green Bay Packers, another storied franchise, have just taken home the Lombardi Trophy, which is given to the winner of the Super Bowl. In a taut, entertaining game they defeated the Pittsburgh Steelers, who won the Super Bowl just two years prior. Meanwhile, the Redskins watched the playoffs from the luxurious comfort of their couches, having posted a 6-10 record. The Packers and the Steelers have very similar philosophies. The philosophy of the Redskins is a world apart.

It wasn't always this way. For years, the Redskins "built through the draft," meaning they selected talented young players out of college and nurtured them through the years, forgoing offering big contracts to free agents. And for years—even through ups and downs—the Redskins were on balance a big success, winning four NFL championships and appearing in more Super Bowls than all but four other teams. During their glory years—the first reign of Hall of Fame coach Joe Gibbs—the Redskins' philosophy was very similar to that of the Steelers and Packers today. That is, build through the draft, show loyalty to your players and coaches, put character first, value longevity, put the organization above the individual, and be focused on the future as well as the present. All of that changed in 1999, when Daniel Snyder bought the team.

No one questions Snyder's passion to win or his willingness to spend to be a champion. Since he has owned the team, he has been willing to stroke huge checks to free agents who have demonstrated prowess on the field but worn out their welcome with their former teams due to character and work ethic issues.

No one illustrates that more than Albert Haynesworth.

By all accounts, Haynesworth is a physical rarity—a fast, athletic, hulking defensive lineman, capable of dominating a game. He also has a well-deserved reputation for being immature and a distraction to his teammates.

Before the 2010 season, Haynesworth was signed by Snyder to an extraordinarily large contract, in spite of his reputation. From his earliest days on the team, Haynesworth was a headache for the new head coach, Mike Shanahan. Shanahan had enjoyed a long run of success as head coach of the Denver Broncos and was known to demand strict discipline of his players.

At first, Haynesworth could not pass a physical fitness test. For several weeks, Shanahan demanded that he pass the test before he could play. The relationship between the two deteriorated and became the focus of the team. Then Haynesworth refused to play at his position in the defense Shanahan had installed, which was different than the defenses Haynesworth had played in throughout his career.

Immovable object, meet irresistible force. Haynesworth soon refused to even talk to Shanahan. Shanahan held firm. And eventually the coach suspended the player for the last four games of the season, leaving a $120,000,000 benchwarmer to languish on the sidelines.

Coach doesn't trust player. Player doesn't trust coach. Owner makes decisions based on physical prowess alone, not alignment with mission or character. Fans trust no one. Team loses.

On a high-performing team, the leader has to insure that the members trust each other and act in ways congruent with that trust. One of the most important aspects of getting to this point is being willing to bring conflict into the open when it surfaces, rather than pushing it back into the ground.

Provoking Healthy Conflict

A recent study examined the most successful teams in the world and found that they almost always have two primary characteristics: a great sense of humor and high levels of conflict! Why is healthy conflict helpful? Because it forces deeper thought, a willingness to examine our own positions, the need to forcefully articulate our positions, and a focus on larger issues that transcend the individual. Unhealthy conflict destroys. Healthy conflict energizes and leads to richer outcomes. We'll explore this in detail later in the book.

Healthy teams have conflict. A lot of it. This is for two main reasons. First, talented people have strong opinions and are willing to articulate and defend them. Second, conflict leads to clarity and is an indicator that a team is thinking things through, and willing to experiment with different approaches and open to new ideas.

Strong leaders will deal with conflict in at least three ways.

They will **provoke** conflict. Conflict over competing values is a good thing as we saw earlier. Sometimes leaders have to go out of their way to stir up healthy conflict so that values can be exposed and agreed upon. In his seminal work on leading through change, John Kotter talks about the role of the leader in actually creating dissatisfaction, which then leads to a desire for change. Similarly, you will find yourself—as a team leader—at times needing to create good conflict to get a team through a stale patch or over an impasse that has come because people aren't talking about what really matters.

They will **guide the team through** the conflict. Once it is on the table, the leader must make sure that the conflict stays about the values and that the team stays focused on the end goal, the mission.

And they will **leverage the conflict** to accomplish a bigger purpose. Ask yourself, "How has this conflict made us stronger? What lessons have we learned? And where do we go from here to build on what we have learned and experienced?"

Inspiring High Commitment

Mike Krzyzewski is the head basketball coach at Duke University, where he has won multiple national championships. He is also the head of USA Basketball and won the Olympic Gold Medal in 2008 in Beijing.

Everyone acknowledged that "Coach K" was a great college coach, one of the all-time greats. His Duke teams are known for their discipline, intelligence, poise, and unselfishness. But some skeptics questioned whether he could coach an Olympic team loaded with millionaire professional superstars. In college basketball, the coach is everything, with unquestioned authority and power. In professional basketball, the superstar athlete in whom an owner has invested many millions of dollars will almost always win in a conflict with a coach.

But Coach K and his team took home the gold medal and, in so doing, he demonstrated how a leader fosters a culture of high level, nearly all-consuming commitment from his team. These principles work whether you are coaching a team, leading a work group, or chairing a volunteer committee.

We've talked about it a lot so we won't belabor it here, but Coach K *chose the right team.* He was questioned for the balance of his team—choosing three point guards, for instance, when two were normally enough. But as he said later his key was choosing the right teammates, not the most talented players. He chose players who he believed would work together, and work for a higher cause.

He also *made the whole appealing.* Kobe Bryant, a member of the team, is known for scoring immense amounts of points. But at the first Olympic team practice Bryant did not even take one shot! This was because Coach K, in private meetings, had impressed upon Kobe that if he subordinated his own scoring to the team, great things would ensue. In game after game, the players deferred to one another, and as a team they were barely challenged.

Like Paul Azinger, Coach K also *managed relationships.* It is vitally important that a manager know each of his employees well—their talents and traits and the places where they are likely to struggle and succeed. But this knowledge alone is not enough. Once you know your team you will be able to pair them with others, or place them in sub-teams where they will have the best opportunity for success.

Say one of your team members is a Communicator. They could sell snow cones to Eskimos. And they love to talk. In fact, they never stop talking. You would not want to pair them on an important project with another Communicator, because they would probably try to out talk each other and end up accomplishing very little! You would be more likely to pair them with someone who excelled at administration and follow-through so that the brilliant ideas and clear communication could be harnessed into successful results.

In his writing about the Olympic experience, Coach K made it clear that he always communicated the mission of the team with great clarity. They were there for one reason only—to win a gold medal for the United States. This enabled the team to focus with unrelenting will on that one goal—and made it possible to winnow out every other distraction that would have harmed high performance. High performing teams are absolutely clear about their purpose.

It sounds like a "soft" concept, but Coach K knew that the ultimate determiner of high commitment was whether or not he *believed in his team*. "In all forms of leadership—whether coach, CEO, or parent" he wrote, "there are four words that when said can bring out the best in your team—I BELIEVE IN YOU."

Knowing that your leader believes in you will drive you to work harder, think more clearly, sacrifice more... all based on the security and fulfillment that comes from starting with acceptance, not having to earn it.

Provide Honest Feedback and Focus on Results

When you offer someone the gift of accountability, you are honoring and respecting them, not micro-managing them. Accountability says "I believe that you have the capacity to do this thing and I believe that this thing is important." Important enough that, together, we need to make sure that we are driving the process forward.

A key component of accountability is giving feedback. Here is how you can do that:

1. Provide feedback immediately, whether the feedback is good or bad.

2. Provide feedback specifically, with immediate options for enhancement, improvement, and correction.

3. Provide feedback systematically, with planned times for give and take.

4. Provide feedback with the good of the person in mind.

5. Provide feedback that is focused on the goal of the team.

You'll also want to be accountable yourself. This is part of trust.

And you will want to insure that when results are in and goals are met that you celebrate!

OK, you have selected your team and focused them on the task. You are practicing the principles of great team-building. Now you are ready for the third aspect of the Tactical Option, the one that truly separates good enough leaders from great ones—empowering the people on your team!

Chapter Eight
Empowering People

Susan was quite simply one of the most agitated team members we had ever met. We were seated in a windowless conference room with her and as we talked—well, as *she* talked—she drummed her fingers on the table and left her styrofoam coffee cup untouched. Her nonstop talking was a litany of complaints about one man—we will call him "Joe Mentee"—a man who had been assigned to lead a team of which Susan was a part.

Now, it was an honor to be selected for this team. Susan and Joe both worked for a very large public engineering firm which had just been awarded a potentially game-changing contract. The work would put them in touch not only with leading figures in industry but also with powerful government agencies and even the general public. The contract had the potential to secure the company's position for the foreseeable future and to make careers if it was successful. Or to taint the company's image for a long time if it was not.

Professionally speaking, there was only one choice for who should lead the team—Joe Mentee. Joe was off the charts brilliant, quick on his feet, an engineering genius, and he had all the right experience. He had excelled at complex projects with lots of moving parts involving highly technical challenges. There was only one problem. No one could stand to be around the man.

That is why the company called us in to help with the situation, which was simultaneously full of great promise and great peril.

The question was this: Does Joe Mentee have the people skills to lead the team to success without it imploding?

The early returns weren't good. We received feedback on Joe's leadership style from his direct reports and peers. There was a pattern to the comments. They all began with some variant of "He's brilliant, but...." He's brilliant, but he can't relate to others. He's brilliant, but he has zero respect for anyone's opinion but his own. He's brilliant, but he crushes people along the way.

It was our job to survey the team, analyze Joe's leadership capabilities and make a recommendation about the project ongoing. We believe that people can change for the better, so we didn't envision an outright "no" to Joe; we hoped to coach him along the way. But we sensed that this team of high performers was near mutiny. Susan and others all but said they would quit the team if Joe remained the leader. The very future of the team itself was in doubt.

Why People Quit Teams

It happens. You've selected great team members and done the work of building them as individuals and as a corporate whole. And people still quit, citing boredom, burnout, a "better opportunity," a whole host of reasons.

But, generally speaking, team members don't quit if they are truly empowered. For a leader exercising the Tactical Option, empowering your team is crucial. Let's talk about what that means and how to do it.

Let's start with a definition. When would you know that your team members are empowered? In a nutshell, empowerment is measured by how willing people are to give us the very best of their discretionary effort. Discretionary effort is what it sounds like—excellence offered at the discretion of the one giving it. It is not about bare minimum standards or even incremental improvement. A person giving discretionary effort is not just punching a clock or marking time—they are investing in something, "paying it forward." Someone giving discretionary effort is going above and beyond the call and teams full of people who are giving discretionary effort are the teams that win!

So, how can you insure that your team is full of empowered people giving their discretionary effort?

We'll start to answer this question by peering from the underside—why exactly do people quit teams?

Team Members Quit To Pursue More Attractive Promises

You'll remember that we've talked about the promises teams make to their members. Things such as compensation, time off, continuing education, adequate resources, work hour parameters. When another opportunity comes along that offers better options in this area, a team member may choose to leave. Generally speaking, a Triple A baseball player is not going to turn down the chartered planes, gourmet clubhouse food and drastically increased salary that comes with a call up to the major leagues. Very many people are motivated by higher pay or more attractive hours. When they see more attractive promises or feel that their current team is not keeping its promises, they may leave.

Team Members Quit To Pursue A Bigger Prize

Let's stick with the baseball analogy for a moment. A World Series ring is a bigger prize than playing in the Triple A all-star game. Similarly, many pastors would be motivated by the opportunity to lead a church of 5,000 rather than 500. An awful lot of community college professors would jump at the chance to enter the tenure track at an Ivy League university.

But prizes involve more than professional advancement. There is the prize of increased leisure time with family or the chance to pursue a doctoral degree. There is the prize of a more lucrative network of contacts or the chance to serve a not-for-profit with superior services and resources. For such reasons, team members may quit.

Team Members Quit To Pay A More Affordable Price
Sometimes the cost of being on a team is just too high. Any team member understands that he or she will have to pay a price—time, energy, stress, just to name a few—for joining a team. As long as the price remains bearable over and against the prizes offered, they are likely to stay on the team.

But when the price is too high, a member may decide to stop the billing process.

You've probably experienced this. The hours demanded were cutting into your family time. The stress involved was distracting and threatened your health. A cut in benefits made the long commute seem less than worth it. So you chose to step aside. You left the team.

In our experience, we find that most organizations pay adequate attention to the promises they and their members have made and to the prizes that are offered. Systems are in place to insure compliance and teams are aware that if they break their promises they will lose good people. And they are aware that more attractive prizes elsewhere may lure team members away.

But they are not focused enough on the price their people are being asked to pay.

This was the problem with Joe Mentee's team. The promises and the prizes offered were more than adequate—there were huge incentives for the team in terms of bonuses and a gilded career path were the contract to be executed successfully. But the team members were thinking in terms of the price they would have to pay—could they afford to work with a leader like Joe Mentee?

Here's an example of the price they were considering. Joe invited a few teammates and some clients of the firm to a Major League Baseball game. During the seventh inning stretch, one of Joe's direct reports said something inaccurate about the project to a client in front of Joe. And Joe ripped into his direct report. In front of his teammates. In front of the client. In front of 40,000 baseball spectators.

A third client whom we talked to later said that he actually wanted to punch Joe in the face during that baseball game because his abrasiveness and anger were so over the top. It's a high price to pay to work with and for someone like that.

How about you? Is your team paying enough attention to promises and prizes? We bet they are, or you probably would not be motivated to take the time to read this book. But—and this is a critical question—are you paying attention to the price your team members are paying?

While you are thinking about your answer to that question, let's consider the second big question which frames this chapter:

Why Do Team Members Engage On A High Level?

To Increase The Value They Receive

You may have heard of the old Communist concept of "utility." Workers work because they think to themselves "I'm getting something out of this."

And that is not a bad thing. We want to know that there is a return on the investments we make. If you invest in being a part of a team, sharing in its work, it is right

> **What Motivates People?**
> - Tactical—Rewards and recognition
> - Strategic—Vision and objectives
> - Transformational—Values that transcend self-interest

and reasonable to expect something in return. If it is a job, you expect adequate pay and time off. If it is in a volunteer capacity, you expect access and influence and the rewards of working for the greater good.

But those bare minimums are not enough to keep you fully engaged, totally invested, paying it forward, are they?

Teams that capture the hearts of their members do much more. They give the member the incentive that the value of their investment can grow and grow. The pay increases may be substantial. The opportunity to learn and grow may be unsurpassed. The ceiling may be higher than on any other team I could join. If I know that the rate of return on my investment in this place can be extremely high—and that it is largely up to me if that is the case—then I am very likely to work hard and with passion.

To Return The Value They Receive

Team members who have experienced growing value are intrinsically motivated to give back. For some, gratitude is the motivating factor; for others a simple sense of fairness. But if you have rewarded me in some way significant to me—compensation, advancement, increased benefits, perks, admiration, affirmation— I'll want to say thanks to you. And the best way to say thanks is by offering you (and the team) gifts of my own.

Let's say you identify that one of the members of your team is motivated by words of affirmation and praise—this is important to them and definitely part of the "value" they would enjoy receiving as part of their involvement in your team. You note this and look for every opportunity to build this person up with your words, insuring that they know you believe they are a valuable part of the team.

A crisis comes. The team has to work harder and longer hours than before. But this particular team member rises to the challenge, leads other members and helps the team pull through. The reason why is easy to see—they are returning, with their devotion, some of the value they have received due to your affirmation.

To Share The Value They Receive

This is where the concept of "pay it forward" really comes to bear.

Even though the phrase is best known as the title of a Hollywood movie from 2000, the concept itself has deep roots. The idea is that when you are done a good turn, you respond with another good turn. But the kindness goes not to the person who was kind to you to begin with. Rather, a third party is the beneficiary. When this happens, a ripple effect is set off and the entire community benefits.

It works like this. An empowered team member, who is experiencing an abundance of value, finds himself deeply fulfilled, loyal to the team and its leader and hence motivated to work harder, think more deeply, release more creativity. This creates a cycle of momentum that results in good being done far beyond the compass of the team.

Soon after he moved to Atlanta, Tom Cousins encountered a pastor, Rev. Vernon Broyles. Cousins was not a churchgoer himself, but said that he "liked to hear a good sermon now and again" and so occasionally visited Broyles' church. When Cousins decided to get married he and his fiancée' went to Broyles for counseling. When the sessions were completed, Cousins offered to pay for the pastor's services. Broyles replied that he did not charge for counseling but he would take payment of a different form. If Cousins would attend the church every Sunday for six months, Broyles would consider his debt settled. During that period, Cousins became a committed Christian. For decades to come, Broyles was a steady spiritual presence in Cousins' life. And Cousins and Broyles worked together on a number of occasions to better the city of Atlanta.

According to his friends, Cousins never forgot the debt he owed the pastor and an awful lot of his good deeds were rooted in gratitude for that special relationship.

This is the ultimate goal of team-building—to serve the common good! Deep in your heart, you know that it's not enough just to have your business succeed, your committee realize its purpose, or your team win more games than it loses. We are hard-wired to want to make a difference. There is no greater satisfaction in leadership than when our little part of the world has an outsized influence. But this only happens when we have empowered teams where the individual members are so full of joy and satisfaction that they pay it forward beyond the four walls of their organization.

There was absolutely no chance that this could happen with Joe Mentee's team. Perhaps a few hardy souls were willing to engage for the value they would receive in terms of bonus compensation and the prospect of career advancement. But there was nothing in the dynamic of Joe's leadership that would lead anyone to return or share value.

One incident became, in retrospect, a crucial moment for Joe. He was in a meeting where one of his direct reports was providing a briefing. Joe's peers were also in the room. Halfway through the direct report's presentation, Joe was aware that the report contained some inaccurate information. So Joe interrupted, unleashing a barrage of sarcastic questions and comments at his direct report to insure that the correct information came out. The atmosphere in the room was almost unbearably tense and uncomfortable. But Joe seemed oblivious to that fact.

The next day, Joe's boss called him into his office. "Joe," he asked, "why in the world did you abuse that guy for thirty-five minutes? What makes you think you could do that? And didn't you see me staring daggers at you and clearing my throat to get you to call it off?"

Joe told us later that he was stunned. Not only was he unaware of the fact that he was behaving in a demeaning way, but he never saw his boss' looks or heard him clear his throat! Tunnel vision. And unlikely to lead anyone to return or share value on his team.

Bottom line: empowered teams must be full of people who not only want to receive value but are committed passionately to returning and sharing value.

Now, you probably are thinking "This is great in theory, but what do I put into practice so that I can lead these kinds of empowered teams?" To answer that question, we'll offer a model (The Five Stages of Role Attachment), an inspiring truth (the Intentional Difference Process™), and a checklist for leaders using the Tactical Option to build empowered teams. Finally, we will share with you the one tool we have found most helpful in selecting, building, and empowering teams. Ready?

The Five Stages of Role Attachment

The end result we are all after is the fully empowered team member, paying it forward by sharing the value she has received with the broader community. We're after this because it not only meets our heart's desires but because it insures that we will enjoy leadership success.

But you know that most team members never get there. This is largely because their leaders did not recognize that full attachment to one's role is not automatic. Rather, there is a progression. You as a leader need to know what your team member is going through at each part of the progression and what they need from you. If you fail to do so, your team member may not progress. But if you are committed, you will have highly empowered followers.

Stage One:
Stage one is when a person begins a new role or position. This is the time of Unconscious Incompetence—they don't know what they don't know and are oblivious to the limitations that the surrounding environment will put on their progress. But they are excited to be here! Likely, their emotional state is one of exhilaration—they have been waiting a while for this opportunity and are ready to get it done. During this phase, their behavior will

largely consist of wanting to be noticed, to be acknowledged—to be seen as a success.

During this stage, it is all about coaching that is related to the person. They need directive behavior, to be sure, but the emphasis is on supportive behavior—making sure the new person knows that they can count on you and that you believe in them. Your job is to communicate this, all the while whittling away gently at the unconscious nature of their current incompetence!

Stage Two:

Stage Two is the time of Conscious Incompetence. The member now is beginning to know what she doesn't know and becoming aware of the limitations around her. Disillusionment and frustration begin to set in. This isn't what I thought it would be. This is harder than I thought. I'm not sure I can do this or even if I want to do this. They start to look for a way out that will allow them to save face.

During this stage, what the team member needs from you is help in working around and over the hurdles she is facing, offering mentoring, mission clarity, role clarity, and making sure that the role and the person are the right fit.

Stage Three:

Stage Three marks a turning point. This is the time of Conscious Competence—now, the team member knows what she knows and she is modifying her performance to suit the environmental limitations she faces. She is not yet happy or remotely self-actualized. Her likely emotional state is one of resignation. But her behavioral focus has turned from looking for a way out to looking for ways to survive.

What a team member in this stage needs from you is help in maintaining productivity while acknowledging the existence of competing values and Transformational issues (much more on this in our book's final section). They need to know from you that in spite of the obstacles and hurdles they can succeed.

Stage Four:

Things get a lot better in Stage Four! This is the time of Unconscious Competence, where I don't know how I know... but I know that I do know! Now the team member is consistently outperforming others in spite of the environmental limitations she is facing. Her emotional state has evolved to one of celebration and she is motivated and running hard, looking for ways to do more of what they do well.

At this stage, what a team member needs from you is coaching about how she can increase her capacity to perform, a celebration of her great fit in her role, and the message that she is an owner, not an "employee" in the enterprise.

You might think that this is good enough! After all, most team leaders would be more than happy with a team full of people at this stage. But for there to be true empowerment, a team member has one final stage of the journey.

Stage Five:

This is the stage of empowerment, of Meta-Competence. Now, your team member knows how she knows. She learns by doing, can mentor others, and has finally risen above the environmental limitations. Her emotional state now is one of desiring to reproduce herself in others—paying it forward in the human sense! Her behavior consists largely of learning new ways to help themselves grow and to help others achieve more.

What she needs from you during this stage is partnership—to invent, innovate, break a few rules, develop others, and to exercise the Transformational Option. In this stage, you have an empowered team member. At this stage you have an employee who is unleashing their Intentional Difference™!

The Intentional Difference Process™

Many decision makers within organizations use one of the more popular psychometric instruments to understand people. A great number use strengths-based assessments. Others use personality-type surveys. Some use behavioral-based interviews. Still others use 360 degree feedback interviews. In each case, regardless of the tool or method, organization-leaders are trying to find ways to better know how to unleash the potential of each employee.

They realize as Peter Drucker says: "Of all the decisions an executive makes, none is as important as the decisions about people, because they [the decisions about people] determine the performance capacity of the organization." Understanding the individual and how to position them for increased productivity is a crucial core competency required of any leader who hopes to build successful teams.

Here's why—an empowered team consists of individual members who know their Intentional Difference™ and are committed to meshing their I.D. with that of others on the team. And, on your team, this can only happen if you have a process for managing Intentional Difference™.

Managing Intentional Difference™ results in three things. First, the personal productivity of everyone on the team is increased, because they are functioning within their Intentional

Difference™ (I. D.) and have a clear sense of what their unique contribution is on the team. Second, the relational health of the team is enhanced because everyone knows and celebrates their place AND the place of each team member. And finally, the ability of the group to achieve its goals is maximized.

We realized that this had to be our approach with Joe Mentee. After we did a 360 degree evaluation for Joe, the results were horrific, just as we expected. Our next meeting was with Joe himself and we had to think long and hard about how to frame the meeting. We could come in with a "development plan" borne out of the feedback of his teammates and subordinates. But there was no good news there—it would be a morale-crushing experience for Joe. So, we turned to the Intentional Difference Process™.

Our Intentional Difference Process™ helps individuals and teams learn how they can work together to achieve great things. As we noted before in chapters six and seven, one of the most useful benefits of Intentional Difference™ is how it helps us to identify and own our prevailing talents and traits. The Intentional Difference Process™ helps us optimize the results of our combined prevailing talents, skills, knowledge, experience, passions, and outcomes.

Applying the Intentional Difference Process™ revealed that due to Joe Mentee's talents and traits he loved to chart new courses. This meant that he was good at thinking a step ahead of everyone else and generally coming up with the right answer. His patterns also meant that once he had arrived at the answer he was ready to move on. Tough combination, because it meant that his teammates experienced him as not only a know-it-all but also as someone who discounted their input and shut them down. Joe was so consumed with thinking and doing that he appeared oblivious to the feelings and value of others. He was a million miles away from being the kind of cheerleader of others that his team would need to be empowered and hence to succeed.

It was clear that we had to get Joe to the point where he was using his (very powerful) talents and traits rather than letting them use him. We would have to teach him to optimize his Intentional Difference™.

His talents and traits were formidable. He was wired to get things done. He got them done yesterday. People experienced him as a profoundly impatient man.

His basic character trait of not suffering fools lightly meant that he had tons of knowledge that he was eager to apply right away to get things done. Which meant that he was experienced at steamrolling others in the process. Joe was a brilliant thinking-doing machine who was totally unaware of the feelings he was arousing in others. If he was going to make it as a leader and if his team was to succeed, Joe would have to embrace his I.D. and use it, rather than letting it use him.

Our coaching with Joe was pretty simple. First we taught him that his I.D. included a natural proclivity to ask disrobing questions. Remember how the direct report we mentioned earlier was stripped bare? That was Joe's prevailing pattern running amuck. Second we taught Joe to practice the skill of listening 80 percent of the time, asking questions 10 percent of the time and looking for cues from his audience 10 percent of the time.

We also increased Joe's knowledge on how to handle conflict. We taught him the principles of conflict management

> **The Intentional Difference Process™, applied:**
> Position people to function where they are likely to make more of a difference rather than more of the same.

and actually wrote him scripts for his interactions with the team. It is important that you understand that we were not saying Joe was "bad" or trying to change his personality. Not at all, we were getting him to a place where his I.D. could shine and be used to build an empowered team. Would it work? We held our breath and waited to find out.

The Joe Mentee Experiment

So, we fashioned a game plan for Joe Mentee, encouraged him to listen and ask constructive questions and, most important of all, to focus relentlessly on optimizing his I.D. We were hopeful, but knew that the team faced an uphill battle.

The end results were nothing less than stunning.

Having decided to use his talents and traits rather than let his talents and traits use him, Joe was a transformed leader. He had truly done a remarkable job at the outset recruiting a high flying team of talented veterans and once he decided to support them rather than squashing them they flourished. There were some skeptics at the outset but over time and as the project developed, Joe earned their trust. He was a new man, focused on empowering his team and developing his own unique 5 percent.

The contract was fulfilled beyond the highest expectations and Joe won an award of merit in his industry. The award presentation cited his "leadership, vision, and commitment to his teammates." We have a PowerPoint slide that captures the comments some of Joe's teammates made to him at the end of the project.

They talk about his transparency, the way he built trust, the way he communicated with excellence, the way he removed obstacles from the path of his team, the way he inspired.

Joe Mentee became a truly exceptional Tactical Option leader. And there is absolutely no reason in the world why YOU can't as well!

An Empowerment Checklist

We've thrown a lot at you in this chapter, all of it important. As we end this chapter we want to provide you with a checklist.

We hope you will use this checklist as a way of measuring your progress as an empowering leader—we do, and it is hugely helpful to us! You can think of the checklist as a guide to climbing a mountain!

Provide Clear Direction

An empowering leader defines the task for the team with crystalline clarity. It's not "Do your own thing as long as you are within basic organizational parameters" but rather "See that mountain? We are going to climb it together."

Provide Needed Resources

Nothing is more dis-empowering to a team than not having the tools they need to complete the task they have been assigned. Just ask teachers in distressed school systems. As an empowering leader you will give your people the tools and the resources they need to carry out their assignments with excellence and verve. "Here is the equipment we need to climb this mountain together—everything is safe, secure, of high quality and thoroughly inventoried. Let's get started!"

Provide Coaching, Support, and Feedback

Along the way, an empowering leader is providing constant, specific coaching (Here's how we are going to take the mountain), support (You're doing great—here's what I can give you to help you take your next peak) and feedback (OK, let's set up camp for the night and talk about what we learned today and how we can get better tomorrow).

Provide an Environment of Self-Discovery

As an empowering leader you will spend a lot of time protecting the team by providing just the right sort of environment. What does this look like? Remember the principles of self-discovery we talked about when we were discussing team selection a couple of chapters ago? An empowered team experiences the joy of being able to play out and develop that self-discovery. They are doing what they would already be doing anyway even if they weren't on the team. Only you as a leader are providing an environment that is joyful, stimulating, challenging, and affirming. (Look at how your unique contribution to the team is helping us to scale this mountain! We couldn't be doing this without you and it is amazing to watch you getting better and better at what you are doing!)

Take a moment and inventory your current team leadership. Does your team have the direction, resource, supportive coaching and feedback it needs? How about the environment you are helping to create? Is it fostering self-discovery, enhanced performance, and personal growth?

Bringing It All Together: Intentional Difference Process™

We're almost to the end of our journey together learning more about how to select, build, and empower teams. As we finish, we want to dig deeper into the Intentional Difference Process™, because we believe the Intentional Difference Process™ offers you a winning advantage for every phase of the team leadership journey.

As we mentioned earlier, the Intentional Difference Process™ unpacks whatever psychometric tool an organization uses to understand individual performance.

The Intentional Difference Process™ adds to the value of any personality or strengths assessment tool in two crucial ways. First, it expands your understanding beyond your own talents and strengths so that you can better understand the dynamics of your team as a whole. You'll see where your team is rich in talents AND traits and you'll see areas where you need to shore up your team. Second, you'll also see potential areas of conflict and collision in your team, conflict not born of "personality conflicts" or ill will but from completely natural clashes of otherwise essential talent and traits. In short, you will have a customized understanding of how your talents and traits work in relation to the talents and traits of your teammates.

And that is one of the great, tantalizing questions of leadership—what can our talents and traits look like when we combine them? How much more powerful is the whole than the sum of the parts?

We'll never forget one client case we had at TAG Consulting. For fifteen years, two managers had gone at each other hammer and tongs. They simply couldn't work together without tension. Manager 1 expressed his frustration this way: "Manager 2 slows me down all the time! He's always asking irrelevant questions and woolgathering and slowing the process down. It drives me crazy!" Manager 2 was equally frustrated: "Manager 1 is always running with half-baked ideas, not asking the right questions and one of these days he's going to blow the place up! I spend most of my time slowing him down and getting him to think!"

When we put the team through the Intentional Difference Process™ we learned a very important truth. Manager 1 made things happen, created change, thrived when there was forward momentum. Manager 2 saw the details, gathered information to develop a better plan, thrived when there was a thorough process. In front of our very eyes, Manager 2 said, "So I am not a hidebound jerk after all!" And Manager 1 said, "You're not trying to hold me back and I am not trying to run you over after all!"

A fifteen year rift was healed, they learned to appreciate each other, and the team was strengthened. The insights of the Intentional Difference Process™ can work these sorts of "miracles" in your team as well.

We have found the Intentional Difference Process™ to be the single most helpful tool we know in helping teams re-design task/role assignments to function more effectively. And, as you know, the composition and functioning of your team can make or break you as a leader. Once you have grasped the principles of Intentional Difference™ you will never look at team-building and leadership the same way again!

Section Four
The Transformational Option

Chapter Nine
Discover Your Code

When Carly Fiorina was introduced as the new CEO and chairman of the board at Hewlett-Packard in 1999, she had reached the pinnacle of American business. She was no less than the most powerful woman in the history of corporate America.

She came to HP riding a career with few if any missteps. She had been brilliant everywhere she worked, including sparkling tenures at AT&T and Lucent Technologies. Uniformly regarded as charismatic, decisive and a compelling speaker she wowed the media at her introductory press conference in July.

Carly Fiorina seemed to be the perfect candidate to return the venerable Silicon Valley institution called HP back to its position as industry leader. Until it all fell apart.

Six years later, HP's board forced Fiorina out the door, in a most publically embarrassing way (albeit with a twenty million dollar severance check!). The company's stock price had halved. She had alienated the engineering corps, the very heart of the company. Analysts pronounced her tenure as disastrous and called her the "anti-Steve Jobs" because she had proven unable to work with the brightest technological minds in her organization. The business website *Conde Nast Portfolio* named her one of the worst twenty American CEO's of all time.

What went wrong? Had Fiorina suddenly lost her intelligence, decisiveness, and skill? Not at all. She had simply failed to break the code of Hewlett-Packard. And so the code broke her.

Code: A Definition

Code is the essence of an organization. It has to do with its history, values, practices, assumptions, memories, heroes and stories. It is the stuff that makes an organization what it is. It is the filter that, over time, gently or abrasively, removes everything that is not true to the essence of the organization.

Understood, respected, and leveraged code is a force for good. Discounted, tampered with, or violated code can end careers and cripple organizations.

One of the main tasks for you in using the Transformational Option is to discover the code of the place where you are leading. Are you ready to discover your organization's code?

Ghost Whisperer, not CSI

The detectives on the various CSI franchises live in the world of trace evidence, laboratories, fingernail fragments and DNA found on cigarette butts. They follow the scientific method, sifting, weighing, examining and relentlessly coming to logical conclusions.

It is a great method for solving crimes, but it would be of little to no help in discovering an organization's code.

The code cracker is more like the lead character on the TV show *The Ghost Whisperer*, who uses intuition, instincts and deep knowledge of the inner lives and stories of the people she is trying to help to aid them in bringing their tormented souls to ease and restoring congruence to their lives.

As you discover your organization's code, you are going to be relying heavily on your intuition, ability to ask questions, and willingness to listen long and deeply.

Cracking the Code

Cracking the code is as much art form as it is scientific endeavor. There are certain hard and fast facts about your organization that will point you in the right direction. But you'll need to take some intuitive leaps along the way!

You can start to crack your organizational code (and this applies to community organizations and not-for-profits as well as companies!) by looking at the symbols. Symbols are expressed in five primary forms: myths, traditions, heroes, decisions and visuals.

Myths are the key stories that give flavor and shape to the history of an organization. The founding partners who took out second mortgages on their homes to get the business through a rough spell. The business people on the not-for-profit board who ponied up to save the fundraising drive. The former CEO who left a family vacation to visit a team member's sick child in the hospital. Bill Hewlett and Dave Packard grilling burgers and hotdogs at employee picnics. Sometimes myths tell of moments of triumph; sometimes moments of tragedy. Myths may stretch the truth, but they always say something important about the heart of an organization.

Traditions are collective activities that may not serve a pragmatic purpose but are important parts of the soul of an organization. Think of the early dot coms who offered Beer Bust Fridays to employees putting in a ninety hour work week or of the church with a time-honored Easter worship tradition. Even though they may not be essential to the mission of an organization, you surely don't want to tamper with honored and expected rituals lightly!

Heroes come to symbolize the code of an organization. Bill Gates at Microsoft; Vince Lombardi of the Green Bay Packers; Dean Smith of the Carolina Tarheels; Sam Walton of Wal-Mart. Heroes are larger than life figures who embody the heart and soul of an organization.

Decisions are those "turning point" moments in the past that may not have seemed important at the time. Years later, however, we understand them to be pivotal. The time the founder decided to give the reigns over to a new CEO. The time a board turned down a request to merge with another company.

Visuals are the outer face of an organization. Think ambiance, architecture, logo, letterhead, e-mail signature lines and office furniture. All say something important about the code of an organization.

If you do a thoughtful survey and list out your organization's myths, traditions, heroes, decisions, and visuals, you will be on your way to cracking the code!

During the East Lake transformation, Tom Cousin's team members were code crackers extraordinaire. And the best of them was Mayor Shirley Franklin. We'll devote much of Chapter Ten to seeing how Franklin demonstrated remarkable elegance and dexterity in leading from the Transformational Option. For now, let's just recall that her first priority—evidenced by going to the same meetings and having the same conversations again—was to crack the code of East Lake Villages. Until she had done that, all of the persuasion and fine planning in the world

> **A Problem is Transformational When...**
> - It impacts multiple stakeholders
> - It is complicated by deeply held values
> - It will result in loss for someone
> - A solution may not be found
> - You have a history of failing to solve the problem
> - People are overly dependent on the authority figure
> - It is related to your code

would have made absolutely no difference.

We also should remember that the entire East Lake effort was an outpouring of Tom Cousin's personal code—notably the core beliefs that poverty and dysfunction are not acceptable, that one must never give up in a worthy endeavor, and that people will eventually want to do the right thing.

Eva Davis had her strong personal code as well: personal pride in the face of adversity, a desire to keep power from outsiders who might threaten her community, and a fierce love for her neighborhood.

Clashing codes, to a certain extent. And no progress would have been made had each code—corporate and personal—not been understood and honored.

The Litania Sports Group Story

One of our clients is the Litania Sports Group, the result of a merger of two companies. Gill Athletics was the industry leader in manufacturing equipment for track and field events—hurdles, pole vaults, javelins—you name it. Gill was a privately held company with a hundred year history of being one big family for its employees. Porter Athletic Company was the world's leading outfitter of gymnasiums.

But Porter had fallen on hard times and was on the verge of bankruptcy several years ago. A merger with Gill was in their best interests, it appeared. Hence the new entity of Litania Sports Group.

David Hodge, the CEO, asked us to come to Champaign-Urbana, Illinois to assess the newly merged company and offer suggestions for how to make the new arrangement work. While the company remained highly profitable, very efficient, and saw an increase in market share, something didn't feel quite right and he was concerned.

Our first day onsite, we conducted focus groups, like we always do. We were struck by the fact that we heard the same question over and over: "Who do I work for? Gill? Porter? Litania?"

Gill and Porter had very different reporting structures and deployed managers very differently. These structures had become part of their respective codes. And the newly merged entity had not given adequate thought and consideration to the differences. But people don't violate a code they are used to readily and organizations are largely intolerant when a code has been dishonored. Now, everyone was frustrated.

Another question we heard was "How do we brand ourselves?" The two companies had two very different brands—again, part of their respective codes. And there had been inadequate time given to taking those code differences into account when positioning the new company.

What to do? We started with a breakout exercise where we had the senior management answer a series of questions, such as:

- Describe your most positive memory of your time working for this company.

- Describe your most meaningful work experience over the course of your career.

- What are the best, but most difficult, decisions this company has made in recent years?

When the groups came back together, they were shocked to learn that each group had answered the questions almost identically. We were starting to crack the code of the newly merged company. Five themes emerged:

- Overcoming challenges

- Having fun

- Camaraderie

- Achievement

- Growth

Previously, we had taken the leadership team through our Intentional Difference Process™. Reflecting a unique profile, the leadership team's top five talents or traits were related to:

- Achievement. These people thrive on checklists and getting things done.

- Responsibility. People with this talent keep their promises and feel a personal obligation to do so.

- Exploration. These people have fun exploring options and figuring out new ways to get things done.

- Learning. These people get bored easily and want to learn new things—especially short projects in new areas.

- Relationships. People with this talent develop close personal friendships and have rules around who gets in their inner circle.

Just as we finished the core values exercise, David excitedly pointed out that their top five team talents or traits matched, line by line, the five themes that emerged from the code exercise.

Core Values	Intentional Difference Process™
Overcoming challenges	Responsibility
Having fun	Exploration
Camaraderie	Relationships
Achievement	Achievement
Growth	Learning

Alignment is a beautiful thing.

The intersection of core values and team talents or traits revealed the essence of the code of the new company. That all came clear in about thirty seconds (trust us, our job is not always this easy!). And now Litania has clarity and renewed hope to build upon.

Now What?

Okay, you have engaged in the thought and emotional energy necessary to begin cracking your code. What do you do with your new knowledge and deepened understanding as you lead from the Transformational Option?

Never Violate The Code

Refusing to honor code was at the core of Carly Fiorina's downfall at Hewlett-Packard.

We were at Hewlett-Packard in 1998, a year or so before Fiorina stormed into the place. We interviewed entry level employees, middle managers, and senior executives. We wanted to know HP's code. HP's code is intertwined with its founders, Bill and Dave, who had started the company in a home garage. They were down to earth, approachable, humble, personal extroverts who promised lifetime job security and a down to earth workplace. These and other values had become enshrined in the HP Way, a written expression of much of the company's code. The central theme of the HP was very radical for its time. Bill and Dave believed this: that employees' brainpower was the company's most valuable asset. They were one of the first ones to introduce all-company profit-sharing plans which gave shares to all employees. They were at the leading edge of providing job sharing, flex time, and even tuition assistance.

We asked the employees what the HP Way meant to them. The answers ranged from "respect for employees" to "you can't lose your job." Each person had a different way of expressing the HP Way but the code was crystal clear: Employees are our most valuable asset.

From the outset, she didn't seem to fit. She took to traveling with an entourage and left the room immediately after speaking to employees instead of mixing and mingling like Bill and Dave had done. She made it clear that she was going to make big changes. Her first strategic move? A merger with Compaq in 2001.It was a very public battle, vigorously opposed by director Walter Hewlett, Bill's brother. The impact of the merger? Fifteen thousand layoffs! A direct violation of the HP Way. Worst of all, she publically and privately disparaged the HP Way, sometimes in not so subtle ways.

She rammed through a misguided acquisition of Compaq and eventually the Board fired her. But, really, the Compaq deal was mostly an excuse to jettison a leader who had alienated employees and shareholders alike by violating and disdaining Hewlett Packard's code.

Take it from us. Even if big changes need to be made in your setting, do so in a way that does not violate organizational code. Here's why.

Code is neither good nor bad. It just is. But its "is-ness" (if that's a word) is immovable. Code orients how team members think of themselves, their work or volunteer service, and their place in the organization. Code is a sacred thing. You won't gain anything by trying to change it. You might lose a lot if you don't understand it or if you violate it. We always want to understand and honor code.

Keep Working To Crack The Code

We've talked a lot about cracking code, but it is not like cracking a safe. We mean, it is not a one and done venture. Think of code as the pot of gold at the end of the rainbow. You can see it from here, you can get tantalizingly close to it, but you will never fully crack the code. Too much of it is caught up in intangibles—how in the world do you crack myths and rituals?

But we should never stop trying! Because in pursuing the code we create trust, stability, and understanding and we provide a sense of continuity and honor.

Remember That Code is a Right Brain Deal

Once we were speaking at a conference for executives of not-for-profit organizations. During a coffee break, an intelligent, well spoken, highly placed not-for-profit leader approached us with a lament and a question.

Her lament was that something in her organization seemed out of sync. There were things going on in her not-for-profit that were incongruent with its stated mission and values. But she couldn't seem to put her finger on why.

"I have to be honest with you. I just don't get this whole code thing. What IS it, exactly?" We asked her to tell us more.

"In my work, I try to get to the unshakeable facts," she said. "I need to understand budgets, balance sheets, donor history, and the demographics of the communities we are serving."

We asked her several questions in response. "Do you ever ask people about their memories of the organization or its previous leaders?" "Do you ever think about the architecture and decor of your offices?" "Do you ever ask what stories have become larger than life or whose lives your organization has impacted the most?" This fine leader gave us a blank stare in return.

See, her assessment was all left-brained—concrete, data-driven and logical. She was leaving out all traces of intuition, memory, story. And it is in these latter places that code is revealed.

Our culture places a premium on defining reality through logic. Left-brained stuff. But code is all about identity, not numbers on a ledger. And, at its essence, identity is right-brained. Code is deeply embedded in the symbols that draw people together in community and create meaning. Code is a narrative force, not a logical system.

You should not be frightened to take intuitive leaps as you lead from the Transformational Option. Be willing to let myths, stories, and rituals guide you as you pursue congruence with core values and mission accomplishment!

Select Leaders Who Fit The Code

Nothing can derail a leader faster than selecting team members who do not fit the organizational code. This will never, ever work. And it will give you heartburn as it is in the process of not working!

The television journalist Roy Firestone was once interviewing Duke's Coach K. He asked what he believed to be a perceptive question, and he got a surprising twist of an answer.

Coach, he said in effect—Is your job to win national championships or to coach players?

Coach K replied that is was neither. "My job," he said, "is to protect the culture and values."

He went on to relate the story of a star athlete who was considering jumping to the NBA after only one year. Part of the code of Duke basketball

Who is Responsible For The Work?
- Tactical—The leader
- Strategic—The leader and the people
- Transformational—The people

is that getting an education is an important thing. The "student-athlete" is taken seriously at Duke. Coach K steeled himself to have a difficult conversation with a player who had dollar signs dancing in his frame of vision. But he discovered that he didn't have to because other players had already taken their teammate to task, reminding him of the program's values and persuading him to stay in school. This is what happens when a leader protects, articulates, and honors the code.

What a paradigm shift! Our first task is not to manage people or resources, make a profit, provide a good or service, or attract charitable contributions. It is to protect the code.

At least, that is the first job for a leader exercising the Transformational Option.

And then, after that? Ah, here is where it gets tricky. And fun!

Chapter Ten
Develop Your Adaptive Capacity

We had been looking forward to this day for a long time. An entire day to spend with the key players in the East Lake transformation! High caliber leaders all, people with resources and connections who had leveraged their influence and gifts not for personal gain but for the common good.

Over a wonderful dinner in downtown Atlanta the night before our meeting, we talked about the day ahead—what to expect, what sorts of questions to ask, what outcomes to anticipate. Our goal was to get to know intimately a great case study for the Transformational Option. And we discovered that our team shared one assumption in common—that Tom Cousins would prove to be the exemplar of the transformational leader.

We were wrong.

The next day we filed into a pleasant conference room for our interviews. Their surroundings were like the people themselves—comfortable, of high quality, but down to earth and unpretentious. We set up our laptops, legal pads and digital recorder and prepared for a long and thoroughly satisfying day of interviews and conversation. We spoke with Chuck Knapp, Tom Cousins, Carole Naughton, Greg Giornelli, and others. We missed the face to face meeting with Shirley Franklin, who had been called out of town.

Each person we interviewed was incredibly impressive and demonstrated their strengths. But we scratched our heads wondering which one of these people had truly used the Transformational Option. We heard lots of strategy and tactics from this talented group. But not much that fit our understanding of the Transformational Option. A few days later we were able to get Shirley Franklin on the phone and all became crystal clear. She was the transformational leader we had been looking for.

Things We Think We Know

When it comes to leadership, we tend to think we know a lot of things. Certain things about leadership seem to be self-evident, as obvious as the nose on our faces. But over the years we have seen that some of our most cherished beliefs about leadership are dead wrong. Do you hold any such assumptions?

Leadership is a Noun

We assume that leadership is a thing. A thing to be exercised, a thing to be mastered, a thing to be studied, a thing to be perfected. After all, if you look "leadership" up in a dictionary, it says "noun." So, it must be, right?

Leadership Requires Positional Authority

You have heard it said a hundred times. Maybe you've said it yourself. "I'm not sure how they expect me to do this job. I have all of the responsibility, but none of the authority. It's impossible." Unless you have positional authority—final say over major decisions and the ability to tell others what to do—you assume you can't accomplish any sort of important task, whether in the vocational or volunteer arena.

Leadership Concerns Power

People running for political office say "I want to serve," but we know what they really mean. It's about acquiring and using power, right? In your case, you assume that you will exercise power for good but you know that if you are going to lead you must have a measure of power.

Okay, okay, we all (mostly) buy into the idea of servant leadership these days. By that we mean the idea that the job of the leader is really to serve those she leads as together they accomplish a greater good. But, still, even a servant leader must be able to move some mountains just by saying so, right?

Leadership is About the Leader

We don't trust leaders much in our culture these days, but we want to. And we assume that when people are good leaders it has much to do with talents or traits they possess—intelligence, political savvy, superior training, emotional intelligence, the right connections. After all, not just anyone can lead; it takes a special someone. Right?

But what if these truisms aren't actually true? What if leadership isn't a thing after all? What if leadership requires neither authority nor power? And what if leadership has very little to do with the superior qualities of the leader himself?

Leadership is an Activity

We've been influenced greatly by the Harvard professor Ronald Heifetz, a good friend of us at TAG Consulting. No one writes better or more wisely about what we call the Transforming Option. And no one makes a more compelling case that leadership is not a noun, but rather an **activity**—a process engaged in by both leader and team.

And that process can be a high stakes drama! "Leadership arouses our passions," says Heifetz, "because leadership engages our values." We don't want you to miss this crucial point: leading from the Transforming Option is all about values, often values in competition. That's why the Transforming Option is the most challenging sort of leadership you can engage in. That's why it offers hope and potential for the greatest impact. So, practically, what will you be doing as you lead from the Transforming Option? Let's look and see...

Know What Kind of Authority You Have

We've all done it. By "it" we mean assume that leadership is only possible if you have authority. The kind of authority that comes from a position of power. The kind of authority where you can marshal resources or change equipment or overcome bureaucracy solely because of the position you have.

And it is true that positional authority can be useful. But for the Transformational leader it is never enough, because positional authority does not guarantee that you have the power to get thing done.

Heifetz distinguishes between formal and informal authority. Formal authority comes from a title or from a position. "Chairman." "Boss." "Owner." "Employer." Informal authority comes from those being led. If you have informal authority it has been offered to you by those you lead. Ultimately, informal authority is the only kind that matters.

Imagine that you are a middle school teacher. You have your education degree, you have your classroom, you have your favorite chair in the faculty lounge. You have a position—you are a teacher. And you have a captive audience—a room full of middle schoolers. But do you really, truly have authority?

On the one hand, your students can relate to you attentively and respectfully, partnering with you in the journey of learning. They can choose to trust you, to listen to you, to do their homework and not be disruptive in class, to engage with passion and interest in classroom discussion.

Don't Yell Louder

One of our colleagues at TAG says "if yelling at your kids doesn't work, yelling louder will probably work less." If one motivational session didn't create buy-in for your vision, don't hold more sessions. This is probably a sign that you are facing a transformational issue, which requires a different approach.

On the other hand, they can sit sullenly. They can pass notes and propel spitballs. They can refuse to be quiet and never turn their homework in on time.

In either scenario, you have formal authority. You are a "teacher." But only in the former scenario do you have informal authority. And only in the former scenario is anything of lasting value likely to happen.

As a matter of fact, great things can happen even when you are under house arrest.

One of the most inspirational leaders in modern Asia is the Nobel Peace Prize winner Aung San Suu Kyi, the Burmese opposition leader. Born the daughter of the man who negotiated Burma's independence from Great Britain in 1947 she seemed destined for greatness, even living under the oppressive Burmese military junta, which has controlled the nation for years.

In 1988, Suu Kyi returned to Burma from abroad to care for her ailing mother. In August of that year, a massive pro-democracy protest erupted and Suu Kyi was given the chance to address a rally of a half million people. Soon after, she founded and became the General Secretary of the National League for Democracy, which to this day remains perhaps the most vital force for freedom in Burma/Myanmar.

These noble activities inspired the wrath of the junta and they soon cracked down on Suu Kyi. Remarkably, she spent fifteen of the twenty-one years between 1989 and 2010 under house arrest, denied access to allies and friends and separated from her children and husband, who died of cancer during that time. Repeatedly offered freedom if she would only leave the country, she refused choosing to stay with her people in her nation.

Denied any sort of positional authority—cut off from her colleagues in the National League for Democracy—she leads from a place of moral credibility. Like great Transformational leaders do, she has reframed the very nature of the democracy debate in Myanmar.

"It is not power that corrupts, but fear" she declared in a famous speech. "Fear of losing power corrupts those who wield it and fear of the scourge of power corrupts those who are subject to it."

If the people of Burma/Myanmar ever realize their freedom it will be due in large part to this woman who exercised the Transformational Option from a place of no positional power at all.

During the East Lake transformation, Shirley Franklin—like Suu Kyi—knew that formal authority was not enough. If they wanted to, the Tenants' Association and its proxy, Eva Davis, could stymie her at every turn. Her experience, résumé and former titles—all impressive—would not amount to a hill of beans unless the residents gave her the gift of informal authority. This is a gift that only leaders can give.

As you think about the current leadership challenges you are facing, ask yourself this question: Do I have formal authority, informal authority, or both? You may have the title or the job description, but do you have the trust and ceded authority of those you are leading—the "consent of the governed" to use the words of the founding documents of the United States?

If you don't have informal authority yet, don't lose heart. Rarely is the gift given all at once. The gift is part of a process and comes as a response to a leader who has demonstrated great trustworthiness.

Identify The Transformational Challenges And Define Reality
"The first job of a leader," Max DePree wrote, "is to define reality." When you are leading from the Transforming Option you will find that it is essential to say it like it is when you speak of your group's challenges and opportunities.

When your followers know that you understand their challenges and those of the team as a whole and that you are not shying away from confronting them, their trust in you will increase—they will edge towards being more eager gift-givers of the informal authority you need to lead effectively.

When we are not realistic about the challenges and obstacles we face our followers are left to wonder if we are clueless, incompetent, or simply dishonest.

You know this instinctively, right? As an aspiring leader, it is part of your D.N.A. to know what challenges you are facing, what resources you have at hand, what support you are due to receive and what to expect. If you are going to climb Mount Everest, you want a Sherpa who clearly explains the exertion required, the danger that is imminent and the supplies that are needed. What you don't want is a guide who says "Hey, I got this—no biggie. A light windbreaker and a liter of bottled water should do it. Now, can I have your check?"

Particularly when we face a crisis—misconduct of a team leader, daunting financial shortfalls, the loss of a key customer or constituency—our temptation is to downplay the severity of the challenge in hopes of keeping the team together and motivated. But your team already knows. Let them know that you know too, and that you are all in this together!

Shirley Franklin did this brilliantly in East Lake. Her model of community relations, she told us, begins with "Be consistent in your message. Explain to people without reservation and without condition what you are proposing to do. I knew that in order to work in this community you had to work with the established leadership, which is not a bad thing. I knew that Ms. Eva Davis was a force to be reckoned with." And she knew she had to tell the truth at every turn.

You've learned during our time together how to distinguish tactical and strategic issues from transformational challenges. Now is a great opportunity to put your new knowledge to work and in so doing speak truth and reality into your team's life!

Identify All Of The Stakeholders

As consultants, we see our first job with a new client as making sure that we know who all the stakeholders are. And it is our job to give them input into the consultation. This means we have to know who is engaged, why they are engaged, and what their stake in the game is. This takes the form of interviews, focus groups, and surveys. Sure we get good information. But more important, we engage all key stakeholders before introducing any changes. If we skip this first step, we will have to deal with it—painfully— later. So we never skip it. And you won't either, as a Transforming Option leader!

Who has skin in the game? Who has reputation or compensation or position invested in the outcome? Who is likely to gain and lose influence? Who stands to win the most? To lose the most? Who's not sure? Who are all the key players, internally and externally, who might be affected by your leadership? These are Transformational Option questions.

As we interviewed the key players in the East Lake transformation it became clear that divining who the key stakeholders were was both all-important and enormously complex. Fortunately, Cousins and his team made the critical move of recruiting Shirley Franklin, with her background in community organizing. As it turns out the principles of community organizing include an enormous emphasis on identifying those who are invested and involved in the change at hand.

First, Franklin understood that the problems at East Lake were complex and systemic. "My sense of why communities disintegrate is a combination of poverty, few opportunities for legitimate work, failing schools and the disintegration or absence of anchor institutions like not-for-profits, faith-based organizations, the United Way and the like," she told us. "It is the disinvestment in a community that eventually causes it to collapse into complete dysfunction."

And these complex problems meant that if there were to be a transformation, there would be many different people and constituencies who would be affected. "You had problems of poverty," Franklin says. "You had problems of education. You had problems of federal regulation around public housing that made it seem impossible to improve your community. Then you had the people (residents) themselves, who were divided over what it was that they wanted their community to be."

Think about how many stakeholders were invested in East Lake. Residents. Educators. Government employees. Bankers. Political office-holders. Developers. Grant writers. Religious leaders. Social workers. Just to name a few. Here is the thing to see—if even ONE of those groups had been ignored or de-emphasized the entire transformation could have come down like a house of cards.

On April 20, 2010 there was a traumatic explosion on the oil rig Deepwater Horizon, killing eleven workers and beginning a nightmarish three month period that resulted in nearly five million barrels of oil being spilled into the Gulf of Mexico and incalculable damage to sea life, the environment and countless small businesses.

The rig was leased by British Petroleum (BP) and its then-CEO, Tony Hayward soon became the public face of the crisis. Unfortunately, his highly successful career was marred by the next three long months of gaffe after gaffe.

Early on, Hayward failed to define reality. Soon after the spill he told a reporter "We made a few little mistakes early on."

As it turned out the statement was untrue on its face—BP was revealed to have made a number of catastrophically bad decisions which contributed to the tragedy. But even if it were strictly true, it was less than true to the reality of dead and injured humans, a savaged ecosystem, sludge-soaked marshlands and thousands of fishermen and small business owners who had lost their livelihoods.

But it got worse. Trying to empathize with the victims of the disaster, Hayward made a statement that still causes us to scratch our heads. "We're sorry for the massive disruption it has caused to their lives. There's no one who wants this over more than I do. I want my life back."

> ### The Solution Becomes the Problem
>
> When applying a tactical solution to a strategic or transformational problem, the "solution" becomes the problem. Instead of confronting three employees who are chronically late returning from their lunch break, a manager institutes a time clock for all two hundred employees. There is an immediate revolt. The "solution" (time clock) became the "problem" (revolt). If the manager had simply confronted the three tardy employees, he would have saved a lot of heartache. But he avoided his own transformational issue—he wants to be liked and hates confrontation. As a result, the solution became the problem. In your organization, what policies or solutions have been put in place that perhaps made sense at the time, but have since become problems?

Millions recoiled at the thought of a petulant, multi-millionaire CEO of a major publically-traded corporation put upon by being kept from time on his corporate jet, vacation homes, and luxury yacht.

Hayward had failed to consider the stakeholders involved and to empathize with their plight. And within months he had been ushered into an early retirement, replaced as the CEO of British Petroleum.

Expose Competing Values

Part of reality is that in transformational leadership, values will collide. When this happens it can be scary. You're tempted to minimize differences, to paper over conflict in hopes of arriving at your destination unscathed.

Don't. You just can't.

Because when you not only acknowledge, but actively work to expose competing values you are opening the door for truly transformational change. And this is what you really, deep down, want.

In our experience, this is where leaders who are closest to success often fail. It is hard—sometimes painful—to acknowledge that conflict comes from more than personality differences and miscommunication, but that fundamental values are in opposition. However, great leadership emerges from this tension. Ask Shirley Franklin.

All of the different players had different values. Left unexamined, the assumption of all those involved would be that their values—dear to them—were misunderstood and threatened by those they deemed to be in competition. But this white noise masked the fact that underneath the competing values was a common desire—for the wellbeing, peace, and prosperity of the residents of East Lake Village. If the values in competition were not brought to

Dealing with Organizational Threats

- Tactical leadership protects the organization from threats

- Strategic leadership anticipates threats

- Transformational leadership discloses threats and competing values light, faced down together, and seen for what they were, no communication, clarity, or change would have been possible.

Lead Change At A Rate That Is Tolerable

Change brings distress. You know this from experience. Even if the change is to the long-term benefit of all concerned it is still hard, scary, and threatening in the very beginning. It has to be done, but you have to introduce change at a rate that won't overwhelm those involved.

You've seen leaders who failed to do this. A pastor who knows his congregation has to change to meet changing times and so throws out the pews, hymnbooks, and choir without warning and finds himself looking for another church. An ambitious young manager who says "We need change around here!" changes virtually everything, and alienates everyone who reports to him, short-circuiting his career path. The volunteer who assumes leadership of a not-for-profit board and whose first action is to recommend changing the bylaws of the organization, without warning and without consultation, only to find the other board members resign with no explanation

Matt Doherty was one of the rising stars of college basketball coaching when he took over the reins of his alma mater's program at the University of North Carolina. Talented, brash, and unafraid to face down Coach K just down the road in Durham, Doherty assumed stewardship of a program that had been led by the winningest coach in college basketball history (Dean Smith) for thirty-six years and then for three years by Smith's long-time assistant, Bill Guthridge.

Doherty had played for both men, was a passionate Carolina man, and was eager for the challenge. But he was a much younger man and was convinced that change was needed in the tradition-laden Tar Heel program. Perhaps most of all, he burned to make the program his own.

So, in his first few months in charge he did the following:

- Refused to keep any of the members of the previous, beloved coaching staff, including the best point guard in Carolina history, Phil Ford.

- Dismissed several long-time members of the program's support staff, some of whom had served for decades.

- Took down photographs of several legendary greats from the program which were hung prominently in the basketball program's offices.

Doherty made the program his own, to be sure. It may even have been the case that some of the changes were necessary. But without getting buy in from key stakeholders and involving them in the change process, Doherty lost all of his relational capital. Just three years later—after the team's record was an unheard of 8-20, the coach was summarily dismissed. According to insiders, no one in the Tar Heel basketball office shed a tear.

Another key principle of community organizing that Shirley Franklin employed in East Lake was this one: "Ask for input. Be open to input. Then be open to modifying what you are doing based on some experience this community has. Then design a plan with the community to move toward execution and outcome."

As with every other aspect of leading from the Transformational Option, leading change at a tolerable rate creates trust. Franklin knew that without trust, progress was a no-go. "My job," she told us, "was to be sure that the general sense in the community was one of trust so that the tough negotiations could take place." This was especially important so that Eva Davis could feel that she had room to compromise and negotiate. "If there was not a general sense of trust then she would have been working against the very people she was trying to represent."

In our work, we evaluate where our clients are in the process of change and offer counsel and advice that matches their speed. If a client is still coming to grips with change we don't offer a proposal for wholesale transformation. Our job is to help the client be prepared to do the work themselves, ultimately. Part of leadership may mean offering only small steps, or simply raising the right questions.

We want to be clear here. Leading change at a tolerable rate does not involve appeasement or a failure of nerve. Leaders often see the change that needs to happen more clearly than others and have to be prepared to pay a price—the price of resistance. But, look at Shirley Franklin's words, "based on some experience this community has." Every group has its story. As you get to know the story of your team you will be in a much better position to determine the pace of change that is tolerable and to bring that change about skillfully.

Give The Work Back To The Team
This is one of Heifetz's great insights—the people doing the main work of leadership are the people themselves, not the leader.

Yes, we know that sounds counterintuitive, even bizarre. Hang with us for a moment.

If the job of leadership belongs to the leader alone, the span of change and impact will be limited to the capabilities of one person. But if the job of the leader is to frame the issues, define reality, expose competing values, insure that the right questions are being asked, and provide resources for the people to mobilize then the end whole will be greater than the sum of its parts.

Let's say you go to the doctor with a backache. After examining and questioning you, the doctor is convinced your back is simply sore because you helped a friend move last weekend. "I don't even need to prescribe anything for you," she says. "Just take a few Advil and take it easy the next week or so." Quick fix, and your only work is to take the medicine.

But what if the doctor comes to believe that your backache is from something more serious—a herniated disc? Now, there is more work involved for you. Even if you have surgery, you will have to agree to some lifestyle changes, stretching exercises, core development, and better posture. More of the work for the "cure" belongs to you.

Now, what if the doctor suspects an even more grim prognosis—cancer? And what if after scans and exploratory surgery the cancer is revealed to be severe, perhaps life-threatening? No "cure" is immediately available and your prognosis is not good. Now, MOST of the truly important work belongs to you—decisions about how to spend your remaining time on earth, important conversations with loved ones, choosing how to allocate your resources and provide for the education of your children, choices about experimental treatment or hospice.

In this last case—admittedly not fun to think about—the role of the doctor (leader) is limited. A skillful doctor at this point knows that she most likely cannot "cure" you; her greatest contribution will be to frame the issues and raise the questions and provide the resources you need to make the big decisions and changes that will result in an enhanced quality of life and emotional and relational health for you and for your family.

This is transformational change and these are the kinds of choices faced by leaders employing the Transformational Option. This is what Heifetz calls "adaptive work," where the leader's job is not to decide, mandate, or command. Rather the task of the leader here is mobilizing followers to accomplish important work themselves. This is your "adaptive capacity." How does this happen?

We've covered a good bit of this ground, but this is a good time to summarize the behaviors that you, as a leader choosing the Transforming Option, are insuring that your team actually does the work:

1. Build rapport and create a safe environment for everyone.

2. Distinguish between technical, strategic, and transformational issues and insure that your team sees this clearly. This is part of defining reality.

3. Engage the real issues, not the peripheral ones.

4. Reframe unsolvable problems into ones that can be solved.

5. Manage your personal baggage.

6. Make sure that conflict is about competing values alone.

7. Orchestrate the speed of both conflict and change, leading your group so that both occur at a rate they can tolerate.

8. Mobilize your team to do the transforming work by providing the right questions and the appropriate resources.

This is precisely how Shirley Franklin led during the East Lake transformation. Had she tried to force a technical fix to the problems of the community none of the systemic issues would have been addressed. Had she allowed the issues to become blurred the parties involved would have fractured hopelessly. Had she skirted the competing values the conflict would have been about secondary challenges. But she stayed the course, defined the issues, exposed the conflict, involved all stakeholders and, in framing the issues and values with absolute clarity set up the community to execute the majority of their transformation.

Do you see why Shirley Franklin was a Transformational leader? You won't be surprised to hear that this trait has carried her through her life and career in the days since the East Lake transformation. And her development as a Transformational leader began even earlier.

Franklin grew up in West Philadelphia, part of a close-knit family. She credits her parents with teaching her that each and every person has the responsibility to make the world a better place. They also inspired in her a life-long love of the performing arts; the young Shirley was an avid dance student. And she developed her love of service early on as an active Girl Scout.

From her earliest days, she was interested in what makes people tick and how people can organize themselves for the common good. This interest took her through a Bachelor of Arts program in sociology at Howard University and she matriculated at the University of Pennsylvania in order to earn a masters' degree in the same discipline.

Add to all of this a passion for community organizing and a fire for education and you have the makings of a force of nature— and that was precisely what East Lake needed.

Having observed her firsthand, Tom Cousins and others became convinced that Franklin was the perfect person to lead the city of Atlanta, one of the most difficult municipalities in the United States to govern. At first, she had no interest at all. Position, power, roles—none of these make Shirley Franklin tick. In spite of the backing and promises of support from some of the most powerful people in the city, Franklin resisted. Until Cousins, applying all his powers of persuasion, wore her down.

She ran in a bitterly contested campaign and won. Barely. She received only 50 percent of the vote. In addition to a slender mandate, she faced two huge challenges the day she took office in 2002. The first was restoring trust after the corrupt administration of her predecessor. The second was a breathtakingly large and completely unexpected budget deficit.

So she went to work, telling the truth, building coalitions, asking for shared sacrifice. She took positions which defied typical categories of conservative and liberal. She slashed the number of city employees and raised taxes steeply to combat the deficit. She cleaned up the city's sewer system, a major headache.

She was named one of *Time* magazine's five best big city mayors in 2005. She didn't particularly want to run again, but was convinced she needed to finish the course. She won. This time with **90** percent of the vote.

By the time she left office, Franklin had revitalized the city, won the support of the business community, been selected as a Profiles in Courage award winner and led the National Conference of Democratic Mayors. All worthy accomplishments, but her most important legacy was that she saved a city from the brink by bringing together warring constituencies, convincing them to tackle adaptive challenges, and sharing the credit.

Who knows what comes next for Shirley Franklin? Some have talked about her as a possible future governor of Georgia. She is even occasionally named as a potential candidate for Vice President or President of the United States. Today, she leads the Purpose-Built Communities organization which seeks to accomplish transformations similar to East Lake in other cities. She blogs about her passion for education and Georgia politics. She teaches at Spellman College and co-chairs Atlanta's Civil Rights Center. In all that she does she continues to lead from the Transformational Option.

The East Lake transformation was anything but easy. And because of this the tattered whiteboard Franklin and her teammates took to community meeting after community meeting has become a powerful symbol for us of the perseverance that is required in leadership. That's what we'll look at together next.

Chapter Eleven
Persevere through Conflict

Remember the Coors commercials from the 1990s? We actually got to experience that first hand! As we drove to Pete Coors' office in Colorado, snow blanketed the ground—just like in the commercial. And we were near his home, "somewhere near Golden, CO."

In person Coors is surprisingly tall, gracious, and reflective. But he doesn't fit the image of what you would think to be a hard-charging CEO. He is a man who thinks, and listens, and brings people together. Today, removed from the day to day operations of the brewery, the Chairman of the Board of the merged Molson Coors Brewing company can look back on a career when he had to navigate through conflict more times than one would care to imagine.

Coors told us of a conflict early on in his career at Coors. The relationship between the non-unionized brewery and the AFL-CIO were strained at best. In fact, the union had been boycotting Coors for a decade. Hard lines were drawn on both sides—with the Coors family demonizing the union and the union seeing the brewery as the epitome of corporate callousness towards workers.

But Pete believed things should be different, and he had a radical idea—he would sit down with the head of the union, Tom Donahue.

Coors' family, who also happened to be co-workers, thought he was nuts. His father, the brewery president, was sure that meeting with the union chief would be taken as a sign of weakness. "I suspected that he might be right," Pete told us. "But I also knew that their meeting with me would be a sign of weakness as well. And what harm could come in sitting down to talk?"

Ultimately, relations between company and union thawed as a result of the process that began the day Pete Coors and Tom Donahue sat down at a table together. Two powerful men, representing institutions mired in conflict, had the courage to begin a process of embracing conflict that less secure leaders would have avoided. And they got results.

A Key To Transformation

As a transformational leader, you will face conflict. We know this. You will face a LOT of conflict, as a matter of fact—that is simply the nature of transformational change. What will separate you from other managers or leaders is one thing: what you DO with the conflict!

Your tendency, if you're like most people, is to avoid conflict. But embrace conflict. Don't sweep it under the rug or try to minimize it. "Conflict management" is a terrible phrase. Most "conflict management" seminars teach you how to "manage" the other person by mirroring what they say. "So what I hear you saying is…." That gets you nowhere! As counterintuitive as it may sound, you need to embrace conflict when you are exercising the Transformational Option. But HOW you embrace it is critical.

Tom Cousins' partners in the East Lake Villages transformation could write a graduate thesis on conflict. The locus of their opposition came from the Tenants' Association and its powerful leader, Eva Davis, a woman described by former President Jimmy Carter as a more formidable adversary than Anwar Sadat and Menachem Begin. Ms. Davis was bound and determined not to be taken advantage of by a "rich white developer," not to lose her position of power, and most of all not to have her Association members forced to relocate so that Cousins' could rebuild East Lake.

> **Transformational Questions**
> Sit down with some of your colleagues and discuss the following questions.
>
> - What is the biggest gap between what we say we are and what we really are?
> - What do people hope won't change in our organization?
> - What negative behaviors are driven by positive values?
> - Who really wields the power around here?
> - What happens when someone disagrees with their boss?
> - What things do we avoid talking about around here?
> - What hidden alliances exist in our organization?

At first, Ms. Davis had all the cards. Secure in her position, owed favors by powerful politicians, and convinced that she was right, she could not be bullied or rolled over.

"I remember one meeting with President Carter," Chuck Knapp told us, "when he was just aghast. I don't know if he had ever been talked to like that. She just let them have it."

It became clear that the only way to convince Eva Davis and her followers was by meeting in person. A lot. Over a long period of time.

"I think the people that broke down (the mistrust) over a long period of time were Greg Giornelli and Carol Naughton. They broke it down over many, many meetings and they are the ones who need to get credit for it," Knapp says. "And Shirley Franklin plays an interesting role in all this as a consultant for the East Lake Foundation. She was the person most responsible for getting the school charter approved by the Atlanta public school board. The process was long and it was incremental rather than revolutionary."

But the team finally did win the trust of Eva Davis and her followers. The transformation did take place, even though the odds were stacked against it. The reason why is that the team knew HOW to embrace conflict. Let's look at the two ways that people can handle conflict.

Red Zone/Blue Zone

In their book *Thriving Through Ministry Conflict,* our colleagues Jim Osterhaus, Joe Jurkowski and Todd Hahn argue that conflict must be embraced, not ignored or shunned.

It works like this. Every time we face a conflict of any kind we can choose to respond from either the Red Zone or the Blue Zone. The Red Zone is where we personalize conflict. The Blue Zone is where we focus the conflict around competing values. When personal issues intrude into organizational conflict we end up talking past each other... talking ourselves right into a volatile situation! When we can keep the conflict focused on values and interests that transcend the personal, we have the chance to actually thrive through the conflict because it heightens trust and leads to a clearer vision of our values and goals.

Maybe this chart will help you understand the difference between Red Zone and Blue Zone behaviors:

Blue Zone	*Red Zone*
This conflict is professional	This conflict is personal
It's about the organization	It's about me, or you
The mission of the organization rules	Emotions rule without being acknowledged
I must protect the team and the business	I must protect myself
The conflict is reframed into a discussion of values	The conflict escalates to destructive levels

Where does Red Zone behavior come from? Two main places: our pain and our view of the world. Left unacknowledged, those two mighty forces can condemn us to a lifetime of Red Zone living.

Life hurts and all of us have been wounded at one time or another. Many of us received wounds as children that we spend our lives trying to recover from. When these wounds are left untreated or unhealed they can re-emerge at moments of conflict where a person or situation reminds us of the wounding. Let's say a key figure in your childhood told you that you would never amount to anything, that you weren't good enough. Today, an associate calls the performance of your department into question. Unless you have worked through the wounds you are apt to respond defensively and angrily—after all your self-esteem is on the line, perhaps your entire existence.

On the other hand, if you are aware of your wounds you can make the key decision to step away from the emotion and take your associate's comment as reflecting on the enterprise, not your identity.

Our world views also shape our default Zone. If your world view is that the universe is a place of constant conflict where one must fight to survive and get what one can in a hostile world you will be more apt to default to aggressive Red Zone tactics. But, if you see the world as a place of potentially shared values and aspirations you will be more likely to exhibit win-win, results-focused Blue Zone behavior.

Shirley Franklin is a classic Blue Zone leader. The former mayor of Atlanta, and current President of Purpose-Built Communities, Franklin has a long and distinguished career in government and was a key player in the Atlanta Olympics. And, as we discovered, the East Lake transformation would not have happened without her.

Franklin was hired by the East Lake Foundation to bridge the conflict between Tom Cousins' team and the residents of East Lake Village, led by Eva Davis. She was not alone in the process—Greg Giornelli, Carol Naughton, and Rene Glover would also play hugely influential roles.

When we spoke with Mayor Franklin, she remembered her first encounter with Davis. "She stopped me in my tracks going into this meeting and said that I should just stop coming because there was no way this community was going to allow Mr. Cousins to complete this project and it was a waste of time."

Not to be deterred, Franklin went about putting together a community relations model that defied precedent. The normal course of events would be for a developer to go through all of the proper channels at City Hall and with zoning officials, getting the right permits and permissions. Maybe an obligatory community meeting here and there, but nothing too extensive. Franklin's model was that the process would start with engagement between the community and the transformation team.

"One of the things we did that was a little different," Franklin remembers, "was we went to every meeting of the East Lake neighborhood association and just presented. We would ask for ten minutes on the program, arrive on time, stay for the whole meeting, stay to the end and be respectful of all the other issues. We presented the same plan month after month. This was a community in transition so every meeting would have eight or ten new people who had never heard the plan so we presented it month after month. We had the same white board and you can imagine that it got tattered after a while. It didn't always look as sharp or spiffy as the first few meetings, but the whole idea was just to get people to understand that we were not changing anything. This was not a bait and switch operation."

Shirley Franklin's tattered white board is a powerful symbol of Blue Zone leadership. In spite of personal attacks (at one of the meetings, Ms. Davis told one team member to "Sit your fat ass down"), entrenched opposition and apparently no progress, Franklin kept returning again with consistency. It was not about her—it was about the mission, symbolized by the white board. A leader operating in the Red Zone would have lashed back, or done an end run, or played the political process. This Blue Zone leader never took the opposition personally and she kept the mission first.

So, practically speaking, how can you thrive through conflict as a Blue Zone leader?

Pushback is Your Friend!

This is one of the most basic, yet counterintuitive principles of leading through conflict. When you encounter pushback it is easy to lash back or try to overpower the opposition. It is equally tempting to ignore the opposition or try to get around it. You don't like the pushback because it represents the blocking of a goal that you hold dearly. But it can be your best friend.

Pushback helps you because it shows you that the strategy you are currently implementing is not working. It may be because you chose a wrong strategy or because the timing of the strategy is wrong, but whatever the reason, pushback allows you a chance to step back, breathe deeply and consider alternative courses of action.

Pushback also helps you because it exposes conflicting values, one of the most important parts of the Transformational Option. Transformational leadership is all about clarity around values and one of the best parts of conflict is that, managed correctly, you can see where various sets of values are not in sync.

Those who are resistant to change are going to suspect you, as leader, to respond in Red Zone ways; it is what most people do most of the time. They will anticipate that you will hit back or try to defeat them or manipulate the situation to bring about the change you advocate. What they will not anticipate is that you see their pushback as an ally and welcome it as an opportunity to bring about change the right way. Your welcoming response to their pushback will surprise them and begin to build a bridge of trust.

That is what Shirley Franklin and other team members were doing as they went to meeting after meeting, week after week and month after month. "My job," Franklin told us, "was to establish an atmosphere of trust in the broader community so that tougher negotiations could take place." If she had been bothered or threatened by the pushback she faced there would have been no possibility for trust, the secret ingredient that made the East Lake transformation possible.

Here is how pushback can be your friend:

1. Maintain clear focus—one eye on the moment, the other on the big picture. Persevere and hang in there!

2. Embrace resistance. Move towards, not away from the sources of the resistance. This is a learned behavior, so be patient with yourself. Remember that the voice of resistance is almost always representative of others and once you know what the problem is you can move ahead.

3. Respect those who resist, by monitoring your emotions, avoiding the Red Zone, and always telling the truth.

4. Join with the resistance. Begin together, looking for common values and themes and patterns, looking together for ways the situation needs to change.

Know That You Are Part of the Problem

In our work as consultants we are often called upon to help leaders and their organizations navigate conflict. In virtually every instance, the leader who enlists our help believes that he or she is not the problem. The real problem, these leaders believe, is "that person" or "those people" or "that policy or procedure" or "that division." We've seen a lot of jaws drop when we tell leaders "the problem is you!"

What we mean by that is that in every conflict, every individual involved has contributed to the impasse in some way or another. This is one of the fundamental rules of family counseling—that every member of the family is part of a system that is not working on some level.

We want our clients to continue to employ us, so we finish the sentence beginning "The problem is you..." with an important clause: "so know yourself." If I am aware of my limitations and failures and Red Zone propensities I can lead through the conflict wisely and well.

The writer John Eldredge puts it this way: "What gets in the way is your way!" He means that we all have a way of relating, a manner of leading that we rarely question. And when you don't question yourself you are not conscious of how your patterns of behavior are affecting others, creating resistance, and undermining the very goals you are committed to bringing about. But if you are willing to take an inward look, you can stop being your own worst enemy.

If you can manage yourself—know your heart and mind, understand how and when you can slip into the Red Zone, and put your ego aside for a bigger mission—you have the foundation for persevering through conflict in a way that brings about lasting change.

Navigate Conflict in 3-D—A Blue Zone Approach

What's not to love about movies in 3-D? The technology has come so far that the visuals are crisp and clear without the bulky, cheap glasses. As we write this, we are on the verge of experiencing 3-D television in our homes! Seeing things in three dimensions gives us a bigger, clearer, more lifelike experience of the thing we are watching. Believe it or not, you can manage conflict in 3-D.

At TAG Consulting, we have a framework for introducing change and navigating conflict that gives everyone involved the best opportunity to remain in the Blue Zone. The 3-D Method allows for change to be introduced in three phases: Dialogue, Discussion, and Decision. Each phase has different ground rules and each may take a different amount of time to complete.

Dialogue

In the Dialogue phase, you encourage people to simply state personal opinions without feedback or interruption from others. Each person in the meeting has to share an opinion. The goal is to gather as much information as possible. Your task here is to use whatever authority you may have to enforce the ground rules: no interruptions, no feedback, no reaction. Then stop.

Dialogue leads to deeper understanding. More important, you will discover that you can talk about very intense issues in a healthy way and that, usually, there are more than just two diametrically opposed points of view on an issue in conflict.

Discussion

The discussion phase occurs in a separate meeting some time—days or months after the dialogue phase, depending on how "hot" the topic is. No decisions are made in this phase, but unlike the dialogue phase, you allow participants to agree or disagree with each other.

The goal of the discussion phase is to identify the competing values in play so that you and your colleagues fully consider them when a decision is made. The goal is not consensus. Consensus is rarely achieved up front. Rather, consensus is the byproduct of a series of good decisions. It occurs after the fact.

You may find that your greatest temptation in the discussion phase is to press for a quick decision. But it is important to resist this temptation and let the process play out fully.

Decision

The decision phase occurs after the discussion phase. At the decision point, conflict will emerge, but it will be much less significant because the group has already processed the issue through dialogue and discussion. If this phase becomes too personal, each participant shares the responsibility of helping to make the conversation more objective.

At some point, you will need to make a decision, based on what you perceive is the right direction for your department, team, or organization. This is where you earn your pay!

Maintain Healthy Boundaries

Boundaries are the physical and emotional fences that mark off your personal world, creating zones of safety, privacy and health. Boundaries define who you are, who you are becoming, what you think, feel and do. Boundaries allow you to set your own priorities rather than being subject to the whims of others and they restrict inappropriate access and intrusions.

You may have boundaries that are too fixed and rigid, blocking the flow of new information that challenges your previous experiences, preferences, and prejudices. Or your boundaries may be too flimsy, allowing others to crash in and suck out your values, emotional needs, and identity—you become an extension of someone else.

Unhealthy boundaries go hand in hand with Red Zone behavior. When you are acting from the Red Zone your personal boundaries are always involved and you drag others into your drama.

When you are in conflict, it is essential that you keep your focus and attention on the actual matters at hand. When you find yourself allowing old storylines of your life narrative to color your approach to the task at hand, you are in danger of allowing a flimsy boundary to send you into the Red Zone. And when you see a person with whom you are in conflict as someone other than who they really are (i.e. your nemesis, enemy, someone who is out to sink the organization) you violate their boundaries and sabotage the Transformational Option.

There is a great deal of literature about maintaining personal boundaries. For our purposes, we encourage you to make sure that in conflict scenarios you maintain an acute awareness of the difference between your self and your role.

Your roles—as "manager" or "boss" or "guy trying to change everything around here" are very separate from your self—who you are as "dad," "man," "woman," "spouse," "football fan." In conflict situations you will feel attacked. In those moments, remember that it is your role—something separate from your self—being called into question. Your self is intact. When you respond to your role being questioned as if your self is being called into question, you are in danger of falling into the Red Zone. But when you remind yourself that it is not about you, but rather about your role, you can lead with strength from the Blue Zone.

Seek To Encourage

You'll remember that when Steve Reinemund was leading Pizza Hut into the unchartered waters of home delivery, he encountered pushback and was engaged in conflict. Worse, the strategy did not appear to be working and the company was losing bucketfuls of money each month.

Thinking back on that time Reinemund told us of a Sunday night during that trying time when his home phone rang with the voice of Wayne Calloway, the CEO of PepsiCo, the parent company of Pizza Hut at the time on the other end. This couldn't be good news, Gail Reinemund thought. She was so nervous she dropped the phone on the counter.

Calloway asked Steve if he could come to Calloway's office, just outside of New York City. Steve lived in Wichita. As a matter of fact, Calloway was sending the company jet the next day. As he got on the plane, he told us, he felt as if he were flying to his own funeral. "I thought, oh heavens, it is that million dollars a month we are losing. So I called the head of HR and asked him what was going on and he wouldn't tell me a thing. I knew it had to be bad."

The next morning Steve had to wait a half hour cooling his heels outside Calloway's office, which was unusual for the CEO. His sense of dread only grew during that agonizing half hour. Then Steve was called into the big boss' office.

He sat down across from Calloway waiting to hear that he had been fired. Instead, when he stood back up he had been promoted, essentially as the CEO of Pizza Hut.

Reinemund remembered what Calloway had said to him. "All of your ideas for delivery may not be working but it is the right strategy. Let's work on the ideas, but know that I believe in you. We've spent a million dollars a month getting it right and now is not the time to back down."

Not exactly usual behavior for a corporate chieftain, but then again Wayne Calloway was no normal CEO. "He was a remarkable leader. The thing that he did that was so unusual was that he believed in individuals. As a result you would never do anything that would disappoint him."

When an organization is navigating change and conflict, it badly needs you to be an encourager, a morale-lifter, who sees potential in others and speaks of what they see. This really can be you!

We believe that if you care enough to read this book about leadership, you truly want to invest in practices which are bigger than your own personal ambition. Good leaders call followers to a greater sense of purpose. Great leaders encourage their followers in the middle of the bloody battles that always accompany great endeavors and call out the greatness that lies within each of them.

In his book, *Are You Fascinated?* Ken talks about the four kinds of encouraging people you need in your life. As a transformational leader you not only need these people, but you need to BE these people as well!

First, is a People-Picker. You need someone who sees your appetites, aptitude and ability and knows how to turn those talents or traits into positive productivity. A People-Picker spots talent and desire and reaches out to extend opportunities where the possessor of the talent and desire is in a position to succeed. Are you people-picking in your organization?

Second, is a Possibility-Vendor, someone who calls you to dream big dreams of unlimited potential and call out of you more than you knew was there. Are you dreaming big dreams for people in your organization and "infecting" their minds and hearts with these dreams?

Next, is a Dream-Maker, someone who helps you actually take the next steps in your goals and aspirations. These are door-openers who champion your potential and help you take the next steps. Are you opening doors and scheming to help the people in your organization succeed in times of challenge and change?

Finally, there is a Leader-Leader. These are the people who confirm us as leaders, standing behind us and instilling us with confidence as we face down moments of crisis and conflict. They are the ones who make us believe that we can overcome long odds and achieve great things. Are you instilling wild confidence in the people in your organization?

You probably figured this out as you were reading those descriptions, but each of those types fit elegantly with the Leadership Triangle. The People-Picker is the very definition of an expert and clear illustration of the Tactical Option. The Possibility-Vendor and the Dream-Maker are always looking to and seeking to create the future; they are exemplars of the Strategic Option. And the Leader-Leader is committed to tackling adaptive challenges and leads from the Transformational Option.

The Most Important Thing

It's appropriate that we have ended our time together by talking about encouragement. You see, at the core of it this is what we have hoped to do for you by writing this book. Our great desire is to provide you with encouragement and hope that you can lead with skill, integrity, and success. Even joy!

Leadership is tough. It was tough to transition East Lake Meadows and you have your own tough challenges. But if you have the right tools and choose the right Option at the right time you have the chance to leave a legacy of transformation.

Whatever your setting—business, not-for-profit, church, community organization—if you remember the principles of the Leadership Triangle and choose your leadership options wisely we have hope and confidence that your personal leadership legacy can be one of greatness.

Intermedia Publishing Group

Publishing That Works For You

Do you need a speaker?

Do you want Kevin Ford and Ken Tucker to speak to your group or event? Then contact Larry Davis at: (623) 337-8710 or email: ldavis@intermediapr.com or use the contact form at: www.intermediapr.com.

Whether you want to purchase bulk copies of *The Leadership Triangle* or buy another book for a friend, get it now at: www.imprbooks.com.

If you have a book that you would like to publish, contact Terry Whalin, Publisher, at Intermedia Publishing Group, (623) 337-8710 or email: twhalin@intermediapub.com or use the contact form at: www.intermediapub.com.